Marked by Fire

Marked by Fire
Stories of the Jungian Way

Edited by

Patricia Damery and Naomi Ruth Lowinsky

fisher king press

Marked By Fire
Stories of the Jungian Way

Published simultaneously in Canada and the United States of America by Fisher King Press. For information on obtaining permission for use of material from this work, submit a written request to: **permissions@fisherkingpress.com**

Fisher King Press
PO Box 222321
Carmel, CA 93922
www.fisherkingpress.com
fisherking@fisherkingpress.com
+1-831-238-7799

Every effort has been made to trace all copyright holders; however, if any have been overlooked, the author and publisher will be pleased to make the necessary arrangements at the first opportunity. Many thanks to all who have directly or indirectly provided permission to reprint their work, including:

"341" from THE SELECTED POEMS OF OSIP MANDELSTAM, translated by Clarence Brown and W.S. Merwin. Translation copyright © 1973 by Clarence Brown and W.S. Merwin, used by permission of The Wylie Agency LLC.

Front cover image, *Flight Into Egypt* © is from an original painting by Barbara McCauley, www.cardonahinegallery.com

This life is the way, the long sought after way to the unfathomable, which we call divine.

—C.G. Jung, *The Red Book*, 232.

Acknowledgements

Naomi's recurrent dream:

Naomi and Patricia are in a large country kitchen, cooking up a batch of potatoes to feed the Jungians.

"What could this mean?" we mused over the years. As we began working on this anthology the dream's meaning was revealed—it is our task to feed root vegetables to the Jungians, to provide nourishment from the depths—from the roots of our lineage—to our community. The dream showed us our path. We are grateful for the mystery of the unconscious. That is the Jungian way.

We are grateful for the Jungians—our ancestors, our analysts and consultants, our colleagues and friends—who have helped us cultivate this harvest of root vegetables. We are particularly grateful to our colleagues who join us in this endeavor, who have harvested the root vegetables of their own lives and contributed their soul nourishing stories to this collection.

We are deeply grateful to our publisher, Mel Mathews, whose idea it was that we collaborate, and whose press has brought so much life energy to our community of writers. Patty Cabanas of Fisher King Press is a vital support. We are grateful for her steadiness, her web savvy and her warm spirit.

We are grateful to many whose sharp eyes and clear minds have helped the book emerge: Margaret Ryan, LeeAnn Pickrell, Smoky Zeidel, Leah Shelleda.

We are grateful to Opus House which offered us a magical retreat in which to gather our harvest of papers. Alex Peer and Sharon Adee were gracious and hospitable.

We are grateful for our husbands, Dan Safran and Donald Harms, who have supported this endeavor—listened, advised, consulted, carried bags, driven steep roads, kept the faith.

And finally we are grateful for the magnetic path that led us to the Cardona-Hine Gallery in Truchas, New Mexico, and to Barbara McCauley, whose painting "Flight Into Egypt" expresses the soul of this collection so eloquently, and whose generosity allowed us to make it our cover.

Dedicated to our Jungian ancestors

especially Don Sandner

Contents

Beginning

An opus is needed, that one can squander decades on,
and do it out of necessity . . .

—*The Red Book*

We write this from Opus House in Truchas, New Mexico, where we have come to work on *Marked by Fire: Stories of the Jungian Way.* We are friends and colleagues who have known each other for over twenty years, and we both have strong spiritual connections to the high, pristine desert of New Mexico, and its Pueblo and Spanish traditions of the living divine.

Nevertheless, as is the way with any soul journey, we have been surprised and blessed by several synchronicities (meaningful coincidences). We opened the brochure from El Santuario de Chimayó to find the quote: ***"Life is a journey and you choose to be a pilgrim or a tourist."*** That says it all.

It is fall, and we are entranced by the flaming beauty of the aspens and cottonwoods. Each morning as we sit looking out at the Truchas Peaks, those Precambrian mountains formed by the Ice Age whose core of quartzite is hard and ancient, we light a candle before a carved Virgin Mary we happened upon in a local craft shop, a small piece of quartzite warmed by the sun at her feet. We ask her help, she who knows the penetration of the divine, she who bore the fruit of that annunciation and then suffered the loss of a son. We call to our elders, now ancestors, in this time of the thinning of the veil, late October into early November, asking for their help and guidance as we work. We listen to the suffering of these writers, the mystery of transformation in their lives, and how they found their way to Jung and to themselves.

As we work, we consider these questions: How do those of us who dedicate ourselves to Jung's psychology as analysts, teachers, writers, understand Jung's imprint on our psyches? If we believe, with Jung, in "the reality of the psyche," how does that inform our lives?

The writers in this anthology address these questions in unique and vivid ways. We are at once struck by the diversity and the similarities of their stories. They are very good storytellers, telling about their inner, sometimes secret lives—how each came to maturity and developed a living relationship with the psyche. There are several cultures and countries represented, and yet there is a common theme of being drawn mysteriously on one's path. These are not abstract essays steeped in rationality, but embodied accounts, often beginning in childhood, but always describing a crisis, or a sudden death, or the early abandonment by a father or mother. Reading these papers aloud we are impressed by the resilience and creativity of these writers who were able to navigate difficult fates. They show us that destiny is getting to be who your soul wants you to be.

When Soul appeared to C.G. Jung and demanded he change his life, he opened himself to the powerful forces of the unconscious. He recorded his inner journey, his conversations with figures who appeared to him in vision and in dream, in *The Red Book*. Although it would be years before *The Red Book* was published, much of what we now know as Jungian psychology began in those pages, when Jung allowed the irrational to assault him. That was a century ago.

The papers in this collection reflect how this process continues in the lives of the writers, often with the imprint of Jung. Many times their first experience of Jung came when he or she found a copy of *Memories, Dreams, Reflections,* or *Man and His Symbols,* two of the earlier books that made it to broad populations in the late 1960s and early 1970s. Always there was a feeling of relief, of finding a way when it seemed the individual was lost or dead-ended. Several tell of experiencing the numinous or the divine when this occurred.

These papers portray direct experiences of the unconscious, not those of a "tourist." Jungian memoir—writing that includes and illuminates the inner life, the Spirit of the Depths[1]—is an emerging genre that speaks to the questions Soul brings. How do we answer Soul's demands, knowing that the inner world is more real to her than all our worldly garments? She wants us to track our dreams and visions, to follow our spiritual yearning, to make meaning of the stuff of our lives. Those dark nights, in which you wrestle with a dangerous angel, those bad days on which you are thrown off your path, are more precious to her than all your outer achievements and titles.

---

1 Jung, *The Red Book.*

She wants your obsessions, your nightmares, your wanderings in the wilderness, your ghosts and demons.

Because we have been in the creative fire together we include stories from our time here in Truchas to introduce sections.

Carey Baynes said of Jung's writing in *The Red Book*:

> I always knew he must be able to write the fire he can speak—and here it is. His published books are doctored up for the world at large, or rather they are written out of his head and this out of his heart.[2]

These stories, too, are from the hearts of these writers.

---

2 Jung, *The Red Book*, 214.

Section One
Might of the Earth

Life has always seemed to me like a plant that lives on its rhizome.
Its true life is invisible, hidden in the rhizome.

—C.G. Jung

A Truchas story: We were invited to a brunch yesterday by a group of local artists whom Dan, Naomi's husband, had met earlier in the week. The hostess Trish was guided here by a dream in which her grandfather told her that she needed to paint in the desert. She and her husband Leonardo found an old adobe house overlooking the mountainous, spare landscape, the landscape she paints. "I figure you can think as far as you can see," she says, "so I need to be able to see far off, into the horizon." The land she paints is a Spanish land grant, loved by Spanish families for over two centuries, and embroidered with mysterious rules, boundaries, and shared irrigation ditches. Before that it was home to the Tewa, the Tiwa, and the Towa, all pueblo peoples, and before that, to cliff dwellers who disappeared some eight hundred years ago. P.D.

Patricia Damery: *The Soul is a Riddlemaker: Three Lessons*

Jerome Bernstein: *My Second Tallit*

Claire Douglas: *Bear Creek Farm 1976-1982: Finding Jung–Finding Myself*

The land is alive, sacred and essential in these stories. Patricia Damery awakened to soul on the farm where she was raised. Jerome Bernstein, a city boy, had an experience of merger with the land when he began working with the Navajo. Claire Douglas credits a farm she had in Oregon with saving her soul. That terrain nourished and cultivated her, and helped her find her circuitous way to Jung.

The Soul is a Riddlemaker
Three Lessons

by Patricia Damery

When I was a child, I found an old powder tin of my mother's in the junk pile. It was shiny black with slightly raised red and yellow flowers painted on the lid. I immediately saw the tin for what it was, a treasure box, and set about storing treasures in it, although I forget what these were. I then buried the tin in the chicken yard, drawing a treasure map of the location: four steps toward the house from the old tree snag on the eastern border, then three steps to the right. Occasionally I dug it up, examined its contents, perhaps added to them, and then reburied the tin, drawing another map. I found such satisfaction in this process. I don't remember the last time I did this, but I do remember feeling compelled.

Long after I forgot the powder tin buried in that Illinois prairie, I drove across the great plains and mountains of the West to go to graduate school. Like the fool in the tarot deck, I stepped blithely into the unknown: the early 1970s in California was a far cry from my Midwestern small-town farm life! At the time, I had never heard of C.G. Jung, but I had read Carl Rogers' most recent book, *Student-Centered Learning*. I had just finished one difficult year of teaching physical science in public high school near Chicago with the realization that teaching science was not my path. I wrote to Rogers, asking for a graduate school structured around this style of learning. He graciously sent me a list of schools, most highly recommending an experimental program at Sonoma State University, Humanistic Psychology Institute, calling it a "hot bed of humanism." I packed my '63 Volvo with everything I owned and drove to California.

In 1971, northern California was erupting with new ideas and approaches, and this program fashioned itself as cutting edge. I was fascinated but overwhelmed. Warner Erhard gave a seminar long before he was famous, getting rid of students' headaches using the meditation techniques of Erhard Sensitivity Training, or EST. An art therapist had students paint their bodies; several ran around the campus nude. Dance therapies sprung up everywhere, with anyone who wanted to teach presenting a class. Every Friday, we were introduced to yet another "edgy" development in psychology: core therapy, in which primal conflict was screamed out while being held down by one's classmates; sex therapy, in which sexual hang-ups were openly discussed. My Midwestern sensibilities were blown away! Even the smells of the landscape were different: pennyroyal and bay laurel, tar weed and the dried grasses of the Sonoma County hills.

One of these Fridays, I learned of C.G. Jung through a BBC interview with him, which, to be honest, at age twenty-three and immersed in this hotbed, I found to be boring. Yet I also remember a centering feeling in the sight of this face and the sound of this Swiss German accent. A year into my graduate program, one of my roommates was killed in a bicycle accident. Her best friend gave me my deceased roommate's book, *Man and His Symbols*,[1] a popular book just reprinted with pictures and chapters by Jung and other high-profile Jungians. Here the *archetypal* was named, given form and definition. Here, at last, was a language that addressed a level of experience I had always kept private: my many confounding dreams. Soon after reading *Man and His Symbols* I sought out and read Jung's autobiography, *Memories, Dreams, Reflections*.[2]

The actual story that changed my life was in *Memories, Dreams, Reflections*. At about the same age that I had buried the powder tin, Jung described carving a wooden manikin and placing it in a pencil box with its own specially painted stone. He then hid it in his attic, occasionally visiting it, a practice that he continued for about a year. When I first read this story, something within me was suddenly very awake, something I have come to know as my soul. So I came to Soul's Lesson One: "Pay attention to what compels you!"

Jung stated that this experience of carving and then hiding and visiting the manikin occurred at the conclusion of his childhood, when he was trying to reconcile his inner world with the outer world of school and his friends, in which he experienced himself differently:

> I found that they [his friends] alienated me from myself. When I was with them, I became different from the way I was at home. … It was as if I sensed a splitting of myself, and feared it. My inner security was threatened.[3]

1 Jung and von Franz, *Man and His Symbols*.
2 Jung, *Memories, Dreams, Reflections*. (noted as MDR throughout this publication.)
3 Jung, *MDR*, 19.

Of course, he was also suffering the instability of his parents' marriage, his mother's psychological illnesses, her metaphysical abilities, and then, at age nine, the birth of his sister. "My disunion with myself and uncertainty in the world at large led me to an action which at the time was quite incomprehensible to me,"[4] Jung said of the manikin experience. "The meaning of these actions, or how I might explain them, never worried me. I contented myself with the feeling of newly won security, and was satisfied to possess something that no one knew and no one could get at."[5]

I remembered the angst of the time period when I had buried the treasure tin. I hated school, feeling it ruined me. Now I know I had an auditory processing problem and had trouble learning to read. My class was divided by cliques; the teachers frightened me with their punishments. I did not want to be there. My happiest times were home playing outside with my sister.

I developed a school phobia in second and third grades, often getting sick. There was too much trauma at home, and I feared for my mother's and grandmother's lives. Just before I started first grade, my beloved maternal grandfather died suddenly, my mother became mysteriously withdrawn. My grandmother was diagnosed with leukemia shortly thereafter. This was the beginning of a series of illnesses for my mother and grandmother. Two more siblings were also born during this time, both of whom had medical conditions that required hospitalizations and surgeries. My mother's health deteriorated further while my grandmother was dying.

Those years were a prolonged period of horror. Like Jung, I unconsciously turned to play, to rituals such as burying the powder tin, and to my dreams, to soothe and contain my anxieties. Now reflecting on the traumas of my elementary school years, I saw how play had helped me. In the state of mind in which we play, we are open to the unconscious, in communication with inner—and perhaps outer—daemons offering guidance. Until I read Jung, play's importance remained outside of awareness, yet afforded me the space to follow what was compelling, all the way to California! Jung, and Goethe before him, stated the importance of this kind of direct experience unencumbered by the intellect. Live out what is lively and only then reflect. In the personal inner crisis of Jung's midlife (1913–1916, between the ages of thirty-eight and forty-one), *The Red Book,* his record of his play activity using a technique in

---

4 Jung, *MDR*, 21.
5 Jung, *MDR*, 22.

which he sought images for unresolved emotion and interacted with inner figures,[6] illustrates how much Jung trusted this process.

This is not a popular stance in our culture. As we grow older, we live more and more in our heads. Whatever is received by means other than the intellect is suspect. Jung offered a model for how to attend to images and figures one meets through such activities, which leads to Soul's Lesson Two: "Protect what you receive in this process from disparaging eyes, in yourself or others."

As long as the boy Jung kept his experiences in his play secret, he said he felt safe. I understood this. Big dreams had formed my inner life, dreams I also kept secret. One of the earliest, most formative, of these, "The Dream Pond," I first dreamed at about age three. In the dream I wander from a grassy cemetery west of our small country church into an area where I have never been, an area rich with vegetation. There in a cup of land I find a pond with two mallard ducks swimming in the water. The most remarkable feeling of the dream is that of being inseparable from everything around me: the ducks, the pond, the dense vegetation, the horizon. My body is still my three-year-old body, yet also stretches to the horizons, and I feel completely whole and at peace. This dream opened me to a state of oceanic consciousness that has sustained and guided me into the present. Like Jung, I, too, was having experiences of what Rudolf Steiner would call the "supersensible world,"[7] experiences no one else seemed to have and which I felt would be diminished or discounted if I spoke of them.[8] These dreams and experiences were riddles, riddles that I have come to associate with Soul. Now here was a distinguished scholar telling me his own experiences, similar to mine, and saying,

> This possession of a secret had a very powerful formative influence on my character; I consider it the essential factor of my boyhood …. The little wooden figure with the stone was a first attempt, still unconscious and childish, to give shape to the secret. I was always absorbed by it and had the feeling I ought to fathom it; and yet I did not know what it was I was trying to express. I always hoped I might be able to find something—perhaps in nature—that would give me the clue and show me where or what the secret was. … I was constantly on the lookout for something mysterious.[9]

6 He later termed this "active imagination."

7 Steiner used this term in describing developed perceptions of spiritual worlds perceived by the mind, not the five senses.

8 Damery, "Shamanic States in Our Lives," 71–77.

9 Jung, *MDR*, 22.

And this leads to Soul Lesson Three: "We are rooted in eternity. Most of us don't know it."

Jung spoke of his childhood as having the quality of being absorbed by eternity, afforded in part by the state of mind accessible through this play.[10] When Jung spoke of both his mother's and his two personalities, the temporal one in the present day and the uncanny one with roots in eternity, he named something for me that I had long experienced: the distinction of that aspect of myself that was temporal, in the present and developing, and that which is ancient, capable of communicating with the divinity of all life, with the collective. At age three, I remember thinking, *I know I did not begin three years ago!* Even at that age I experienced visitations of a larger consciousness, visitations that would last a few seconds, that I knew were aspects of my self, but older and larger. I would feel that larger self seeing through my eyes. I consciously *felt* that Presence in me. These moments were precious to me, and when they passed, I would consciously review every time they had occurred before, so I would remember them forever. Now, in reading Jung, I found someone else who reported a similar revelation.

"In the end the only events in my life worth telling are those when the imperishable world irrupted into this transitory one,"[11] Jung wrote in the prologue to his autobiography.

> Life has always seemed to me like a plant that lives on its rhizome. Its true life is invisible, hidden in the rhizome. The part that appears above ground lasts only a single summer. Then it withers away—an ephemeral apparition. When we think of the unending growth and decay of life and civilizations, we cannot escape the impression of absolute nullity. Yet I have never lost a sense of something that lives and endures underneath the eternal flux. What we see is the blossom, which passes. The rhizome remains.[12]

The experience of eternity often involves strange synchronicities. When Jung researched for his book *Symbols of Transformation,* he described reading about the soul-stones of Arlesheim and the Australian *churingas.* It was then he remembered his manikin and pencil box and realized he had participated in a ritual of archetypal

---

10 Jung, *MDR*, 20.
11 Jung, *MDR*, 4.
12 Jung, *MDR*, 4.

dimension, having had direct access to "archaic psychic components,"[13] an early experience of what he would later call the "collective unconscious."

Again, this helped me address Soul's riddle of my dreams. At about the time I was reading *Man and His Symbols,* I dreamed of a young black child who brought me an egg with wings, held delicately in his palms. The image nauseated me, an experience I have come to understand as an indication for me that Spirit is present. Dream snakes visited me nightly, frightening me. As the unconscious heated up with the outer activities of my psychology program, my psychic life screamed. I sampled several therapies before a friend suggested the Jungian analyst who was to lead me from the quagmire of outer chaos into the inner chaos.

Shortly after I had made the first appointment and before I met with my analyst, I had one of the more important dreams of my life, one with deep roots in the collective unconscious. The night of the dream, my husband and I had gone to a hot springs that had no electricity. We went to bed early and I awoke from a dream at 4:00 a.m. having slept eight hours. I got up and wrote down the dream.

In the dream there is a war and devastation and I am trying to escape the police. Two groups of people have united, and a grandmother has died. Her body is laid out in a room upstairs. I try not to look at the body. The casket of a grandfather is also being carried about. I am still seeking escape when I see a black and white picture that shatters. I then understand the only solution is to die, to surrender. I am shot, killed.

At this point I become a man and a beautiful primitive woman comes to me and kisses me. She has blue snakeskin on her neck, a small head, and a huge graceful body. We have sex, unite. Then my parents and family help us find furnishings to reconstruct a house somewhere after the war. All we need is a *manitou* (a huge, black, penguin-like bird) and driving out we see one hiding in the cliffs on our left.

Stunned by the imagery of the dream, I went out into the dark of the early morning hours to soak in the pools of the hot sulfur springs. Emerging from one of the baths, I was shocked to see that I had turned entirely black! Later I learned that the hard water of my home had left mineral deposits on my skin that interacted with the sulfur of the spring's waters to coat my skin, which remained black for a couple of days! This dream was truly about a darkening, a moving into matter, the *nigredo*. After

---

13 Jung, *MDR*, 23.

this blackening experience, I slept another eight hours. It was also the beginning of a terrible depression that lasted a year.

The dream continues to be one that I return to periodically. It was neither analyzed in my analysis nor by any other consulting analyst. In fact, ten years later, when as a candidate I presented it in a seminar group with Edward Edinger,[14] he had little to say about it. I felt shamed and humiliated. I had offered up one of the bigger dreams of my life, and he said almost nothing! I feared it showed something pathological about me, that I should have kept it secret (Lesson Two). In effect, though, the best happened. As Joseph Henderson[15] later told this same seminar group, individuation does not begin until personal analysis ends. This dream remained a riddle for me to live on my own, a significant mystery in my own path of individuation.

Of course, the dream illustrated the problems I was facing as I began analysis. I overvalued the intellect, having majored in both chemistry and math and then teaching both. I often think chemistry's draw for me was alchemy, but that connection was still deep in the unconscious. Science as it is taught in our schools is heady. I identified with those masculine qualities of discriminating thought, reasoning, and linear thinking. My mother was an extraverted thinking sensation type,[16] insisting we children perform well academically, and I had been able to develop my thinking enough to please her.

But I also was suffering. My typology is quite the opposite of hers: introverted, intuitive, feeling. As in the dream, I tried to escape conflict by being "good," pleasing my mother and others by taking a path that was not mine. At the time of the dream, although I had earned a Masters in Clinical Psychology, my ways had not changed. I continued to devalue the feminine ways of approaching life: that consciousness that spreads out through matters of the heart, one in which multimodes of consciousness are acknowledged and valued for their differing fruits, the experience of the eternal. The inner alchemist was obscured in the matter of my psyche!

14 Edward Edinger, M.D., was a well-known Jungian analyst in Los Angeles and interpreter of Jung's work and of alchemical symbolism.

15 Joseph Henderson, who had worked directly with Jung, was a first generation analyst and one of the founders of the C.G. Jung Institute of San Francisco .

16 Jung's typology describes four types: thinking opposite feeling, intuition opposite sensation. We tend to have a primary function that we are best at, plus an auxiliary function that we also have more accessible. The opposite of the primary function would be the "inferior" type, most rooted in the unconscious, and most feral.

My "blackening" in the sulfur springs remains a shocking synchronicity to me. I am reminded of Jung's discussion of the Shulamite of the Song of Songs. "I am very dark, but comely," the Shulamite says,[17] being "the feminine personification of the prima materia in the *nigredo* state."[18] It is only through various alchemical operations that her beauty is released:

> It is clear from this text that the "hidden" thing, the invisible centre, is Adam Kadmon, the Original Man of Jewish gnosis. It is he who laments in the "prisons" of the darkness, and who is personified by the black Shulamite of the Song of Songs. He is the product of the conjunction of the sun and the moon.[19]

Edinger draws parallels with the Shulamite in the Song of Songs to the gnostic Sophia "caught in the dark embrace of matter, … or the Shekinah, the feminine presence of God who is in exile from Yahweh, lost in the dark world, separated from her divine consort. Or she's the anima mundi, the animating spirit that permeates all things. Or, to be completely psychological, she is the primordial psyche in its dark, unregenerate, infantile state as we encounter it in analysis."[20] But what about that word *manitou*?

I had never heard of manitou, but the word was so compelling that I searched indexes. I pondered how my psyche ever came up with this word. The term is not familiar in the English language but is important to native peoples who had populated the area in which I grew up and to the east: the Algonquian-speaking peoples, who are linguistically connected with those of northern California, where I live now: the Wilkit and Yurok and probably the Hoopa and Kurock. Manitou defies translation, perhaps because it is a concept so old and deep-rooted in our Western European culture that it no longer reaches the light of consciousness. It is tempting to equate the word with what Westerners refer to as the Great Spirit, but "Great Spirit" reflects the Western European concept of the divine, one of polarity: Great Spirit—and His creations.

Early Europeans visiting the continent noticed how the placement of so-called manitou stones revealed a harmony of sky and earth through many astronomical

17 Song of Solomon, 1:5 (Revised Standard Version).
18 Jung, *CW 14*, ¶592.
19 Jung, *CW 14*, ¶44.
20 Edinger, *The Mysterium Lectures: A Journey Through C.G. Jung's Mysterium Coniunctionis*, 254.

alignments. In 1636, a Jesuit missionary in Canada, Father Paul Le Jeune, observed that the Indians addressed themselves to Earth, River, Lake, dangerous Rocks, and especially Sky, believing that all of these are animate. Manitou may best describe the animating spirit that is All. Later, Western European interpretations define manitou as "any one of the spirits which control the forces of nature."[21]

This is the paradigm of cause and effect. The Native American view of the world is a whole of which we are one part, and a newer part at that. Humans are not to dominate and change the world, but to live harmoniously in it. This suggests another meaning of manitou, best articulated by James Mavor and Byron Dix, two scientists who studied the manitou stones of New England:

> We perceive manitou as the spiritual quality possessed by every part or aspect of nature, animate or inanimate. Things relate to each other by means of this quality, which may be good or evil, temporary or permanent, fixed or changing. Manitou includes aspects of the natural world that are sensed but not understood.[22]

These men surmised that these stones might be placed in areas to increase the manitou of a place. Many of these stones look very much like a human torso—or penguin! By setting the stone, the human was interjecting self into the equation. Perhaps the placement of the stone established the intention of harmonious balance.

In my dream, manitou was needed for the reconstruction. As a Jungian analyst, I might interpret it to symbolize the transcendent function, that marrying of opposites that were at war. Yet I wonder how the native wisdom of our land can inform me? Sioux scholar Vine Deloria, Jr. describes Westerners' tendency to symbolize what is actually a representation of autonomous spirit. Perhaps finding the manitou is not symbolic but an expression of the dire need for "an invocation or invitation by humans to higher powers to enter into a special kind of event."[23] For me, this "special event" has to do with the relatedness of nature and the otherness of it, while also experiencing myself as a harmonious part of the whole, an embodied experience of individuation. It necessitates an opening of the heart to all, human and nonhuman, or, as the Lakota say, to "all my relatives." For me, it has also meant a *rapprochement*

---

21 Mavor and Dix, *The Sacred Landscape of New England's Native Civilization: Manito*, 2.
22 Mavor and Dix, *Sacred Landscape: Manito*, 343.
23 V. Deloria, Jr., P. Deloria, and J.S. Bernstein, *C.G. Jung and the Sioux Traditions: Dreams, Visions, Nature, and the Primitive*, 197.

with the earth through farming, but this time through the spiritual discipline of Bio-dynamics, a system developed by Rudolf Steiner in 1924, also, as with Jung's work, with a foundation in the philosophy of Goethe.

The soul is a riddlemaker. It says: *Tell me why I do this: why I compel you to bury this tin, why I bring you this egg with delicate white wings, insist you find a manitou.* Soul presents us with questions that must be lived, and in so doing, opens us to the Mystery, determining our lives' paths. As I look back, I see how the sparks of life and lack thereof (Lesson One) led me into chemistry and math and then on to Roger's student-centered approach to learning and across the West to wild California. The road maps were images and dreams I could not explain. I see the importance of eventually developing the capacity to hold the anxieties associated with the imagery and experience on my own, not relying on others—or intellect—for validation (Lesson Two).

I see how Soul's Lessons inform my work as a Jungian analyst. Mystery is the medium. Developing trust in that which washes up upon the shores of consciousness is an important part of healing. To my delight, I have learned that even in my work as an analyst, what Einstein stated is true: *Imagination is more important than knowledge.* In analytic work, play is key to bringing balance and wholeness. A guiding light for my work as an analyst continues to be the alchemical paradox I experienced those many years ago: *when all is black, you know, at last, that you are on the right path.*

Jung was the one to introduce the tools to negotiate that which the psyche gave me. He continues to be fresh and present for me. In *The Red Book,* I see Jung's trust of the psyche, his careful attention to the egg of the image it presents, his knowledge of the need for incubation and protection until the egg is ready to "open." His acknowledgement that the psyche has its own time, rooted in eternity. (Is there collective wisdom in *The Red Book's* fifty years hidden away?)

I take heart in Jung's respect for the fires of eternity. We are so much more than our egos and our egos' agendas. We are Spirit interconnected with all creation. The task of individuation demands an awareness of this creative, embodied experience of the interconnectivity of all life, our hearts, a portal to eternity. In this gnosis the Soul sings: "Set me as a seal upon your heart, … for love is strong as death …."[24]

---

24 Song of Solomon 8:6 (RSV).

References

Damery, Patricia. "Shamanic states in our lives." In *The Sacred Heritage: The Influence of Shamanism on Analytical Psychology,* eds. Donald F. Sandner and Steven H. Wong. New York, London: Routledge, 1997.

Deloria, Jr., Vine, Philip Deloria, and Jerome S. Bernstein. *C.G. Jung and the Sioux Traditions: Dreams, Visions, Nature, and the Primitive.* New Orleans, Louisiana: Spring Journal, Inc., 2009.

Edinger, Edward. *The Mysterium Lectures: A Journey Through C.G. Jung's Mysterium Coniunctionis.* Ed. and transcribed by Joan Dexter Blackmer. Toronto: Inner City Books, 1995.

Jung, C.G. *Memories, Dreams, Reflections.* Aniela Jaffé,, ed. New York: Vintage Books, 1965.

———. *Mysterium Coniunctionis: An Inquiry into the Separation and Synthesis of Psychic Opposites in alchemy.* CW 14. Princeton: Princeton University Press, 1955–56.

Jung, C.G., and Marie-Louise von Franz, eds. *Man and His Symbols.* London: Aldus Books, 1964.

Mavor, Jr., James W., and Byron E. Dix. *The Sacred Landscape of New England's Native Civilization: Manito.* Rochester, Vermont: Inner Traditions International, 1989.

My Second Tallit[1]

by Jerome S. Bernstein

In June of 1969 I began what turned out to be my Jungian analysis. I phrase this event that way because I was only looking for a therapist who was both competent and strong enough to stand up to my stubbornness and bullying (the latter being a word I would not have applied to myself at the time since most bullies see themselves as victims). It was a time of dead-endedness in my life, which presented me with an imperative to begin a new story. Unbeknownst to me, I already had.

I had barreled through a number of therapists in Washington, D.C., where I lived at the time. One day, in utter frustration, I asked a friend if he knew of a therapist whom he thought might be strong enough to stand up to me. He gave me the name of Christopher Whitmont, who happened to be in New York City. The need was urgent. That would have to do.

So I called this Christopher Whitmont (whom I later dubbed "Yoda"), who at the time I did not know was a Jungian analyst. Had I known that, I wouldn't have known what that meant—nor would I have cared. I just wanted a good therapist to help me hold myself together. He answered the phone—no answering machines in those days—and promptly informed me his practice was full, that he was going on vacation in two weeks, and I should call someone else. I told him that I wanted him, not just another name, because I had been told he was a strong as well as competent therapist. I attempted to give him a thumbnail of my history and circumstance. He cut me off and told me firmly that he had no space.

"But, Dr. Whitmont. You don't understand. I chew up and spit out therapists. From what I've heard, I need *you*."

He rebuffed me again. Finally, the bully in me jumped out, and I said very firmly to him, "Dr. Whitmont. That simply is not acceptable!"

---

1 A tallit is a prayer shawl worn by initiated members of the Jewish religion. It is rectangular and fringed at both ends as commanded in the Hebrew Bible. It is worn during morning services and during holidays.

There was a pause. Then he said, "How about two p.m. next Tuesday?"

Agreed. Far from bullying him, instinctively I had said the one thing that really would have grabbed him. He was intrigued. Thus began my road to my self.[2]

In 1968, a friend of mine and I had established a social science consulting firm in the Washington, D.C., area. Due to my dismay at the vacuity of psychological training as I had experienced it in undergraduate and graduate school, I had long since given up on the idea of becoming a clinical psychologist of some sort. So I became a self-dubbed social psychologist. Richard Nixon was about to be elected president.

In 1971, at the initiative of Nixon, the U.S. Congress passed the Indian Self-Determination Act.[3] That legislation effectively ended colonial administration of "services" on behalf of American Indians and gave Indian reservations, through the mechanism of their tribal governments, the authority to administer federally funded programs on their own behalf.[4]

Within two months of that legislation becoming the law of the land, the newly elected chairman[5] of the Navajo Nation called my partner in the consulting firm asking for a consultant who could help establish their tribal Division of Education since he understood that the preservation of the Navajo language was central to the survival of their culture. Until that time it had not been taught in schools on or off the reservation, and for most of the history of the tribe under colonial rule, the teaching or even the speaking of the Navajo language was forbidden by the U.S. Bureau of Indian Affairs (BIA). So I went out for a week's consultation.

On my arrival at the Albuquerque, New Mexico airport, when I reached the doorway to deplane down the stairs to the tarmac and saw the vista before me, I had an out-of-body experience wherein it felt like the land and the sky and its limitless openness and I merged. I had never had an experience like that without psychedel-

---

2 This meant a weekly ride on the Pennsylvania Railroad from Washington, D.C., to New York City and back, 4-5 hours each way, every Tuesday. Amtrak did not exist.

3 Richard Nixon did more on behalf of tribal Indians in the U.S. than any president before or since.

4 Each reservation, by law, has some kind of tribal government, the structure of which has been approved by the Secretary of Interior, who is the official "trustee" of tribal American Indians. Indians who live off-reservation in cities and rural areas, also known as urban Indians, do not fall under this provision.

5 Now known as the president of the Navajo Nation.

ics. I'm not sure I had one like what I experienced in the doorway of that plane *with* psychedelics.

The Navajo reservation lies mostly in Arizona, with pieces in Utah and New Mexico. It constitutes 52 million acres and is about the size of West Virginia. I knew nothing about American Indians, Navajo or otherwise. I decided to go "dumb," since the books I found on the subject were all written by white anthropologists. I figured that if I was going to learn about Navajo culture from a white guy, I would be the white guy I would learn from. I spent a lot of time that week in meetings all over the reservation, mostly listening and being silent. What did they need? What could I bring that could be of value to them? Not much, I thought by the end of that first week. The mission seemed beyond overwhelming.

On my last day there I drove to the Division of Education office in Window Rock, Arizona to pick up some papers and to say goodbye to anyone who might be there. When I arrived there, it was after hours, and there were three men sitting around a tiny government issue desk in a tiny office. I thought they were having a meeting, and I politely said hello and went about my business. Then their spokesman said to me, "We've been waiting for you."

I was surprised, so I sat down. Then he said, "We've been listening to you listen. We think you can hear us. We want you to come back."

I was thunderstruck. "We've been listening to you listen." That notion was to open up a whole new (psychic) world for me.

While on my second trip to the Navajo Reservation[6] I heard that there was an impending meeting between Chinese barefoot doctors and Navajo medicine men to take place in Albuquerque, New Mexico. I knew nothing about either, but decided this was a meeting I could not afford to miss.

That meeting took place in a conference room in the Sheraton Hotel in downtown Albuquerque. There were about a dozen Chinese barefoot doctors and about six or so Navajo medicine men, four translators (Navajo and Chinese), and one Navajo elder who translated some of the dialogue and who seemed to be able to understand the

---

6 All of my trips to the Navajo reservation were professional in nature. I was soon to become The Navajo Nation's registered lobbyist on Capitol Hill in Washington, D.C., as well as their primary consultant for transforming the administration of their education, social, and employment/manpower programs into Navajo programs.

philosophical and religious links between the two Native healing modalities. I was informed that he, the Navajo elder, was also a World War II Code Talker. I didn't know what a Code Talker was at the time.[7]

During a break in the day-long explorations between the two groups, I went out into a long hallway to stretch my legs. I was leaning up against a wall, musing about what I had witnessed that morning and trying to grock how it came to be that I was in such other-worldly surrounds. What was this about for me? What was this about in my life? It all seemed very fascinating, compelling and surreal.

As I looked up from my thoughts, I noticed that the Navajo elder was standing catty-corner from me at the other end of the hallway, about forty feet away. He had a very distinctive face and was a large and imposing figure. We caught each other's eye, and we both stared at the other, caught in a connection that had its own center and definition. It seemed that we gazed at each other for quite a while. Then, quite suddenly, he started walking swiftly toward me. He literally walked right up to and almost into my face, our noses nearly touching. He demanded rather gruffly, "What's your tribe?"

Startled, I blurted out, "Levi."

"Levi," he repeated, and turned the word over a couple of times as he played with the sound. In the same slightly less gruff voice he said, "Levi. Hmmm. Sounds like a strong tribe."

I said, "It is."

He said, "Good," and turned around and strode back into the conference room where discussions resumed. I followed a few moments later.

His name was Carl Gorman. From the moment of that encounter in the hallway of the Sheraton hotel he became my friend and teacher. He was the one who introduced

---

7 During World War II, it was estimated that there were only two non-Navajos who were fluent in the Navajo language. The U.S. Marine Corps initially recruited 29 Navajo volunteers to form the Code Talker unit. These men were assigned to combat units in the Pacific and developed a Navajo code which could be used to identify and locate enemy units and materiel in the midst of battle. Because no one in the war zone understood the Navajo language (outside of themselves), they were able to broadcast openly without having to encrypt messages, which saved much time and many lives. By the end of World War II, the Japanese had figured out the language being spoken was Navajo, but they still could not break the code.

me to Navajo culture and religion. He often referred to himself as my "Indian guide." Carl was my passport through almost any door in the Navajo world until his death in 1998 at the age of 91. It was through Carl that I began to attend Navajo healing ceremonies.[8]

Somewhere in this period I had a dream that I was leading a single snaking line of people—scores of people—up to the summit of a mountain. When I was near the top, I could see that I was near the summit of the Sandia Mountains just outside and east of Albuquerque, New Mexico. I knew it was the Sandia Mountains because I could see clearly to the east and the Great Plains that stretched as far as the eye could see.[9]

This dream struck me as right out of a Cecil B. de Mille movie with Charlton Heston in the role of Moses. It disturbed me a lot. It seemed over-the-top inflated, and I found myself wondering if I might not be a bit crazy with this kind of grandiosity. My analyst,[10] after duly working with me on my associations and amplifications, concluded that this dream had to do with my becoming a teacher of some sort, and that my work might lie in the southwest since the direction of movement in the dream was from east to west. It remained to be seen, he said, what was to occur, when I would begin to descend the other, western, side of the Sandia Mountains.

On my third trip to the Navajo reservation the next month, the man I describe above as the spokesperson who had said that they had been "listening to me listen" invited me to his home for dinner. I went. It turned out his wife was a Hopi Indian, and there was need to go to her father's village at Old Oraibi on the Hopi reservation in Arizona. They invited me to go with them. It was Friday and so Ralph, Sandy, five kids, and I piled into their van, and off we went to Old Oraibi.

Upon arriving at the village of Old Oraibi, we were greeted by a very large wooden sign that read, "White people keep out. You are not welcome here. You do not respect

---

8 See Bernstein, Jerome. *Living in the Borderland: The Evolution of Consciousness and the Challenge of Healing Trauma.* London: Routledge, 2005, 127–129.

9 The Sandia Mountains are the first one encounters coming off of the Great Plains and entering into the Southwest area of the U.S.

10 By then I had registered that he was a Jungian analyst and that dreams were his primary tool for working with me. But I was not to read a single word of Jung for another three years.

and have violated the laws of our people as well as the laws of your own. You are not wanted here."[11] I gulped and remained silent.

It turned out that Sandy's father was a kiva chief, the religious leader of the village. To see him was to know he was a holy man. There was an instant affinity between "Grandpa" and me that remained until his death. He spoke only a little English; I, no Hopi. We became deeply bonded. He saw the holy in me that I had no idea was there.

As it was to be, that night was their Powamu ceremony, Bean Dance, which was one of their most sacred rituals. I was invited by Grandpa to go into the kiva and to witness this ceremony. It was an experience both terrifying and numinous. Sitting on the top of that kiva in biting twenty to thirty miles-per-hour winds at one a.m. in February in the midst of unworldly sounds of roving kachinas that surrounded me was beyond anything I could possibly have imagined or understood. I was in the midst of a world and a psychic realm that truly, literally, was other-worldly. And then when I was so cold I could barely move, it was time to descend the ladder into the kiva, which I did, following instructions about movement and placement in the kiva. The terror of the night suddenly was transformed into a warm and embracing womb in the womb of the earth. I had never felt so at peace in my life.

Then the drums began beating and those strange kachina sounds were now calling down through the opening of the kiva followed by the descent of many kachinas into the kiva. Then began the ceremony.

That night I had the first religious experience of my life. I have no words for that experience except to name it. I was never the same after that experience, which in ways I now understand and do not understand brought me back to my roots in Judaism, from which I had become alienated many years before. For many years, I was the only white person I had ever seen in the village of Oraibi.

The Cecil B. de Mille dream referenced above was followed for the next two to three years by a series of many dreams having to do with healers and medicine people, nearly all of them Navajo or Hopi. By 1973, it was becoming obvious from the direction of my dream process that my unconscious was directing me toward the thought of applying to the Jung Institute and becoming an analyst. I resisted this thought for

---

11 This "quote" is from memory and may not be precise in terms of the literal wording.

several months. It seemed inflated to me and beyond any rational concept I had of myself. And I guess that is the point. It was.

After Bean Dance in February of 1973[12] it was time to fish or cut bait in terms of applying to the Jung Institute of New York. Applications were accepted in the spring. I had enormous difficulty getting my mind around the idea of such a radical turn in my life. I could not make up my mind. There was a deadline. The week before the deadline, I asked my psyche for a dream to give me guidance in terms of taking what felt to me as such an awesome step. That night I had the following dream:

> The dream setting was the village of Old Oraibi on the Hopi Indian reservation. We were standing in front of the oldest house in the village, reputed to be more than three hundred years old. All the villagers from all of time, all the Hopis who had ever lived, were gathered around in a circle. I was inside the circle, not quite in the center. Behind them was a vista that was endless in view. The kiva chief, Grandpa, came to me and brought me a manta (the kind of robe that we often see depicted in paintings of traditional Indians) and placed it around my shoulders. While doing so he said, "This is the Robe of Consciousness." At that moment I physically and psychically merged with the land, and the sky, and the people. It was an experience in the dream that I can only label as numinous and a religious experience. (I still carry the sensation of that moment in the cells of my body.)

The next day I applied to the C.G. Jung Institute of New York.

In 1982, I visited Grandpa at his home in Old Oraibi, the site of the dream. After we talked for a while, I was getting ready to leave. He told me to wait. He disappeared into a space in the wall which I had not known was there and came back with something in his hands. He placed it around my shoulders. It was the manta of the dream. We were standing outside in the very place where the dream drama occurred. I had never shared the dream with him.

In Hopi culture, it is the men who weave. This manta had been woven by Grandpa. Sometime later his family told me that it was the largest weaving he had ever done. The manta is woven in black and white natural and gradations of gray. The colors are natural colored wool; nothing dyed. The black and gray horizontal stripes are overlaid on a white background. The allusion to Joseph's coat of many colors as described in the Book of Exodus in the Hebrew Bible was inescapable. Joseph was the pharaoh's

---

12 I attended every Bean Dance for many years after the first one in 1972.

dream interpreter. This holy man and priest whom I knew as Grandpa had just given me my second tallit from the other side of consciousness. I'm sure he had never heard the word "Jew" in his life.

This event and this dream, and all that followed from it, has guided me/shoved me/demanded of me/pained me/since they occurred. Psyche could not be more of a reality to me than it was then and remains so now. I am now no less in awe of those moments than I was at the time. My two books, and so much of my professional and personal pursuits, emanated from that moment. I say "moment" because it was when my ego was forced to become aware of what it had been resisting. The constellation of these psychic events has been continuous throughout my life. The difference is that now, at 75, I have the perspective to see that so many choices were those that were given. I am reminded of a quote from Schiller: "Freedom is the ability to choose what one must."

About 16 years ago (c. 1995), at another meeting in Albuquerque on native healing, another man and I had an encounter similar to the one described above with Carl Gorman. This man, Johnson Dennison, whom I met on a lunch break, and I have been friends from that time. He was/is a traditional Navajo medicine man. It was during that lunch break that we decided to enter into a collaborative relationship as medicine people between our two healing traditions. He has been very generous in inviting me to attend any healing ceremony I wished to learn from.[13] He has performed ceremonies for me and for some of my patients as well as one of the Borderland groups that I lead. In September 2011, he and a Navajo cultural translator participated in a four day intensive clinical seminar held at Canyon de Chelly on the Navajo reservation, which I led. The seminar was attended by an international group of Jungian analysts and Jungian-oriented psychotherapists. The seminar began and ended with a ceremony for the group performed by Johnson Dennison. The focus of the seminar was to explore the uniqueness and the wisdom of Navajo healing practices and the adaptation of some aspects of their clinical model into the Jungian frame of analytic work.

And, for having said all of this, I still wonder how a fat little Jewish boy from Southwest Washington, D.C., finds himself in the middle of a psychic adventure that is as thrilling as it is daunting and as wondrous as it can be painful. This is my story so far.

---

13 Many are closed to non-natives and some parts of ceremonies are considered to be too sacred to be shared.

Bear Creek Farm 1976–1982
Finding Jung—Finding Myself

by Claire Douglas

I had a farm once in the rainy, coastal hills of Oregon. It spread across a hundred acres or so of marginally arable land tucked amid the once giant timbers of the Siuslaw National Forest. There were hillocks of some decent pines, hemlock, and spruce in need of pruning and tending, two sizeable rock-free fields, a large hay barn, a few out-buildings, and a salvageable 1910 two-story square house with an attic and an almost wraparound porch. Two creeks provided irrigation; a spring, up in the woods behind the house, usually allowed enough water for drinking and washing. A Quaker based community lay up the road from Bear Creek Farm, while further down the Siuslaw River, in Swisshome, high on the riverbank, there was a rare empty building in good condition. This building eventually housed the alternative health care clinic that had become the focus of my energy.

I had fled my East Coast life after a collapsed marriage and very little but continuing violence, and then despair, coming from my and my peers' pro-peace efforts. I'd completed college, belatedly, with a senior thesis: a two-year study on the necessary components for livable, peaceful, and sustainable societies. With a small group of friends, I planned to try to put what I'd learned into practice. Like so many activists in the 1970s, assaulted both within and without, we had grown disillusioned about the possibilities of social change on a national level. Instead, we intended to try to make a difference on a smaller and more personal scale. Because we had medical, child birthing, and social work skills, our efforts were centered on forming a non-government funded health care group in a rural area that lacked doctors. We were idealistic and quite naïve: we thought, for instance, that people just required their basic needs met in order to be good.

My new partner and I had written a short-lived, but well-received, newsletter, *Alternatives in Health Care*, and had spent close to a year traveling around to other centers, looking for a place to give shelter to our vision and/or for other like-minded people with appropriate skills to join us. I had wanted to stay in New Hampshire, but the geography of this northern rain forest captivated me and soon invaded my dreams. I realize now that its misty hills and moist greenery, brought back the solid feeling of safety and home I had felt just before World War II when, loved and tended, I lived for a time in the fragrant woods outside of Edinborough.

C.G. Jung emphasizes the importance of the environment and its influence on a person's development. For instance, in a passage on Paracelsus, Jung wrote:

> Born under the spell of the Alps, …Paracelsus came into the world by character a Swiss, in accordance with the unknown topographical law that rules a man's disposition. … Turning now … to the earth on which he was born, we see his parents' house embedded in a deep, lonely valley, darkly overhung with woods, and surrounded by the somber towering mountains that shut in the moor like slopes of the hills and the declivities … The great peaks of the Alps rise up menacingly close, the might of the earth visibly dwarfs the will of man; threateningly alive, it holds him fast in its hollows and forces its will upon him. Here, where nature is mightier than man, none escapes her influence; the chill of water, the starkness of rock, the gnarled, jutting roots of trees and precipitous cliffs—all this generates in the soul of anyone born there something that can never be extirpated.[1]

So I start this chapter on finding Jung and finding myself with what had once centered me and would center me again amid the hectic business of founding and running a health care center: the land. Before finding Jung, I hadn't appreciated, nor even paid much attention to, my strong feelings for a particular milieu and all it meant to me. Though I live far from it now, the value of my relationship to this land endures, while the years of extraverted work—propelled by a desire to bring about social change—seem pallid and bleak.

So the spell of this particular terrain drew me circuitously to Jung and circled my inner development.

From my bedroom window at Bear Creek Farm, I looked down on a faded red barn across the dirt road that ended at my house, and then over to the fields bordered by mostly second- or third-growth hills. These mist-soaked hills rolled from my far right and from my far left down to meet below the house and barn in a cleft where Bear Creek flowed from seemingly virgin land to where it met Deadwood Creek in a soft, wide open, and most seductive V. Each leg or thigh held one of my two arable

1 Jung, *CW 15*, ¶¶ 2-3.

fields. Crayfish scuttled amid the creeks' stones and often tiny steelhead and fingerling salmon hid under the shade of its rocks. Black bears hunted there as did raccoons, bobcats, skunks, coyotes, and, once, I treed a wolverine. Different birds settled in the creek or on its banks according to their own schedules: Canadian and brant geese, egrets, mergansers, pintails. A large blue heron and a shy, mostly hidden, green heron stayed and nested, patrolling the creek for their families' food, while kingfishers loudly scolded them from the branches overhanging the creeks. In one limestoney place, skunk cabbage gave way to watercress. I gathered it ardently, along with the miner's lettuce, the dandelion greens, the edible mushrooms I recognized from my Cornish, New Hampshire woods: in the spring, morels and puffballs, later, chanterelles and various boleti. All enlivened the food from my vegetable garden. Blackberries grew rampant everywhere and, if not constantly battled, could cover an entire shed or tractor over a particularly rainy season. Rhododendrons and Scottish broom proliferated, as did the ferns. A local farmer put one or two beehives out in the furthest field and gave us some of the field's honey in exchange.

Barn owls and, rarely, a great horned owl nested in my barn along with some Araucana hens that had been abandoned here and whose little blue green eggs seemed, each one, a miracle. Deer ate from my apple trees in the front yard (as did an occasional, and less welcome, young bear). I watched four or five generations of deer make their way over my land; the old mother deer and I grew so close I could welcome her and her family to the apple trees as I sat on my stoop at dawn drinking my early morning coffee. And if I rose and approached them, I had become such a familiar figure, not one of them would flee.

Mists and fogs greeted me almost every morning, and, if it wasn't raining, they made magically shifting forms amid the Sitka spruce, the Western hemlock, and the Douglas fir. "My heart's in the Highlands / My heart is not here / My heart's in the Highlands wherever I roam" was part of a Robert Burns poem I had quoted in my high school yearbook more than twenty years before, as my motto and self-description. I chose it in longing remembrance of my lost Scotland home. I had thought the hardpan Cornish hills of my marriage represented this Highlands haven. Now, I hoped these misty hills would be the answer to my search for home. For a while they seemed a good choice.

The Siuslaw Rural Health Center, which I helped found and managed, was amazingly busy. My partner had been in medical school at Dartmouth when I was teaching at Hanover, New Hampshire's middle school. He finished his training at Harvard, where he was deeply influenced by the twelve radical feminists in the Boston Women's Health Collective who created *Our Bodies Ourselves*—a loving and caring manifesto to personal empowerment and responsibility. He did his residency at Highland Hospital's family medicine program in Rochester, New York. As for me, one of my children was too early married, the other away at school, so I was free to pursue my own interest in women's health. I undertook a social work degree, worked at a Vocations for Social Change office, and wrote for an alternative newspaper. Together, my partner and I started to deepen our interest in more natural and personal child birthing methods. To this end, he did a three-month childbirth rotation at Booth Maternity Hospital and Maternity Home in Philadelphia, while I helped teach childbirth classes and attended some of the teenagers who gave birth there before they gave up their babies for adoption. This interest, like *Our Bodies Ourselves*, led us to become part of a loose network advocating for more humane and natural childbirth. In Philadelphia, we stayed with a Quaker Movement For a New Society group and adopted many of their community building and small group techniques for our future health center.

In Oregon, the medical needs of the mostly poor population we served were immense. We believed we could make a difference. We worked incessantly, even when a second doctor, a midwife, and a nurse practitioner joined us. Because I was unsure of my own value, I decided I needed to keep pace with my partner's exhilarating, but sometimes frenetic, tempo. That was the way to bring about needed change, I thought. But I realize now, that, unconsciously, we were also involved in a competition as to who was giving more of themselves to a righteous cause.

Until we had enough help to take over some of the tasks, I kept the books, did the mental health counseling, the organizing, the planning, the fund raising, the health care and childbirth classes, edited and mostly wrote our newsletter, served as a doula for many births, and filled in where needed (even to racing off up into the hills for the all too frequent logging accidents). We received wholehearted support and badly needed physical help from Alpha Farm, the community up Deadwood Creek Road, who also fed us from their restaurant down river from the clinic. I especially cherished two of the Alpha group and encouraged them when they set out on their own to farm biodynamically, first at Bear Creek, then on more suitable land. I still love them like family.

Outwardly, the Siuslaw Rural Health Center succeeded, mostly, I now believe, because of the backlog of unmet medical needs, but also because we worked very hard and delivered high quality care. Locals, from redneck loggers, to fishermen, to farm folk, hippies, backwoods recluses, and retirees met in our waiting room. My childbirth classes started to fill and the newsletter became popular in large part because I culled home health remedies from our neighbors, naming them as sources and printing their recipes for healthier eating. The local government remanded local drug and alcohol cases to us, and I wrote and secured the first Blue Cross contract for clinic births. We started to pay ourselves more, while still keeping clear of government funding.

However, against all my expectations, and in spite of our shared vision, we failed abysmally in our connections with each other. Envy, competitive one-upmanship, back biting, pettiness—all the vices of pampered and entitled upper-middle class America hitchhiked along with us and threatened to overrun our lives. We had admirable, high-functioning, dedicated conscious selves and engaged ourselves in a noble endeavor. However, we dealt with what I would now call the shadow elements that so surprised us and disheartened me, by ignoring them, or worse, piling them first onto one poor scapegoat and then another! This shadow, disregarded, grew and flourished like rain forest mildew until the rot permeated every corner of our lives. Our clearing meetings, formed to build and support each other and our loving community, became arenas of intolerance, faultfinding, personal attacks, bitterness, and rage.

To make matters worse, one of us turned out to have a long-term addiction to pain medication and looted our dispensary. I thought I'd seen her there, but when I accused her (having done a background check that substantiated my suspicion), I was turned on as the troublemaker. Even when others also found evidence, they preferred to be valiantly loving and charitable. They continued to give her access to her poison until it was too late. The more things seemed to be falling apart, the more I lost my good will and lapsed into a workaholic and unfeeling judgmentalism. Our clinic was humming; it grew more and more busy, and yet was riddled with our individual lapses, righteousness, and faultfinding.

We finally called in a clinical psychologist from Eugene, Carol Judge, to moderate our meetings. She attended them for some months and gave us some invaluable restraints, a sense of boundaries, as well as interpersonal skills. My partner and I knew the theory of community building: Carol provided the example and practice. Thanks to her, things at the Siuslaw Rural Health Center and with the neighborhood started

29

to improve. On a personal level, she enriched my life as well, and we gradually became close friends. However, late the following year, she was diagnosed with an advanced case of ovarian cancer. In spite of my increasingly hectic life, I kept her company as much as I could. Toward the end of her life, she asked me if I knew of Jung. Not much, I replied, though he seemed more human than Freud. But I listened when she said that, after she recovered, she planned to see a Jungian therapist, Mary Lee Fraser, who had studied in Zurich with Jung and retired to Port Orford, Oregon.

Carol died soon after this. I felt as if I had lost my only link to womanly sanity and calm. I covered my grief by working harder than ever and becoming, alas, even more unfeelingly driven and judgmental. My body, however, decided it had had enough. My period turned into a seemingly endless flow. The doctors recommended rest, but my partner relied on me, his battle companion, to stand arm-in-arm with him on the front lines. He, therefore, wouldn't or couldn't see my true condition, and he was, after all, the doctor. The bleeding worsened, and I developed a nasty tenderness deep in my right side as well. Now the doctors wanted to operate to stop the bleeding while my gynecologist worried that, like my friend Carol, I might have developed ovarian cancer! I ended up with no cancer but did need a hysterectomy that forced me to rest—at least a bit. Any of the clinic's work that could be brought home was deposited on my bed, and so even my rest became somewhat of a joke. I felt deeply guilty for failing to support our dream and failing to do my fair share of our work. I also felt that my weakness betrayed my partner, our shared vision, and our love. My woman's body had cheated on my feminist stance and, as in the marriage I'd fled, I failed to make the grade.

I started to have nightmares, especially a repetitive one where my much-loved partner and companion on this venture appeared hopped up and crazy. He would seem normal, but then, in these dreams, suddenly start racing up and down the walls and ceilings all over the clinic and the house, sometimes frantically calling out to me. After a particularly vivid nightmare, I phoned Mary Lee Fraser and asked if I could keep my friend, Carol Judge's, appointment.

I bless the day I tore myself away from my many duties and made the drive from Swisshome to Florence, and then on Highway 101 south along the coast past Reedsport and North Bend, Coos Bay and Bandon, to Port Orford—Oregon's oldest and most westerly port. Or if you go by rivers: past the mouths of the Siuslaw, the Umpqua, the Coos, and the Coquille (music to my long-repressed poet's ear)—their waters never quite quiet, but sometimes angry and turbulent as they burst out into the Pacific Ocean.

At my first visit, I found my future analyst outside high on the ocean bluff in front of her house standing by an enormous skull and rib bones of a whale! She looked like an ancient mage conjuring spirits from the deep. A few peacocks, geese, and top-heavy turkeys, unpenned, wandered around her. Inside, countless books and ashtrays seemed to have strewn themselves haphazardly throughout the house, while a growing family of ten or twenty (or a hundred) canaries flew freely around. I had entered an enchanted world. If I'd known fairy tales better then, I'd have sworn I'd found a modern day Mother Holle—equally eccentric—who not only lived life according to her own rules, but might possibly be odd enough to be able to hear me and help heal me. I was wary but enthralled.

My only experience of prior therapy had been in 1958, at some crisis early in my marriage, when I stayed in New York City for a few months to consult a Freudian. He had the usual, deeply hurtful, prejudices against women current at the time, but worse, he seemed deeply bored by me. He ordered me to free associate while he spent much of our hours on the phone consulting with his stockbroker or, sometimes, manicuring his nails. I had such a low opinion of myself that I didn't demur.

Mary Lee Fraser, on the other hand, wasn't bored at all. She took me seriously, but preferred my dreams and intuitive side to my accomplished, but to her, wearisome, persona. I formed the habit of driving down on a Friday or Saturday to see her for a few hours in the late afternoon. I'd found a $25 a night motel on the ocean bluffs nearby, so I slept to the healing susurration of the ocean waves below and then saw her for another two hours the next morning—or until she thought we'd satisfactorily plumbed my dreams. She seemed to have all the time in the world for me, something I'd not experienced since leaving Scotland. To my amazement, she valued both my dreams and their dreamer. I reveled in the attention she paid to my every aspect, and I started to regain some long lost spontaneity and naturalness. She taught me, through her example, to value wholeness rather than the perfection I considered mandatory, and that we needed to pay attention to all my aspects including so much that I'd been taught was shameful.

After our first meeting, she regarded me with some bemusement and declared she had no idea what to do with me: I was obviously what she called a thinking type, but not at all masculine. She pulled out a stack of old mimeographed volumes and handed them to me to take home. They were a seminar about what she called Jung's analysis of a thinking type woman.

In the seminar, Jung described the woman's thinking as so highly developed that it repressed, or was used in place of, her feeling and intuition. Without these as bridges, her thinking isolated her and caused her to live in a sort of ivory tower. Jung went on to say:

> Now, her inferior feeling is the foundation of that *tour d'ivoire* and has secret passages, underground ways where it can escape, and because it is blind like a mole one does not know where it will turn up. But you can be sure it establishes connections somewhere . . . If you are perfect in your perfectly differentiated function, then underneath something escapes into the night.[2]

These mimeographed volumes of Jung's *Visions Seminar* were the beginning of my immersion in Jungian thought. I cannot think of a more difficult place to start, as they threw me into admiration of Jung and disagreement with him—especially with his statements about the woman author of the visions (which seemed in contradiction to what he said elsewhere). My continued need to make sense of, and sort out, this red hot love/hate relationship with Jung became the source of one of my first published essays a few years later.[3]

I will always be grateful to Mary Lee Fraser for freeing me to find and wrestle with Jung and Jungian thought in my own beginner's way. She seemed to have no agenda nor did she make Jung (or herself) the arbiter of any given Truth nor his words sacrosanct (which would have killed my budding development). Rather, she let me and my dreams use Jung's writings to help me wrestle with him and shape my own sense of Jung's value, then, hesitantly, my sense of my own value. She was always there to contribute what she felt and thought and to confront what she termed my animus'

---

2 Jung, *The Visions Seminar*, 7.

3 Claire Douglas, "Christiana Morgan's Visions Reconsidered," *SFJLJ*, 8, 4 (1989) 5-27.

> In an odd quirk of fate, or should I say, synchronicity, my involvement with the *Visions Seminar* continued and eventually led me to discovering their author, her papers, and her side of a fascinating story. I first wrote this reconsideration of the visions, then a biography of the visioner: Claire Douglas, *Translate this Darkness*, New York: Simon & Schuster, 1993. Finally, I edited the "old mimeographed volumes" of the visions: C.G. Jung, *The Visions Seminar*. Claire Douglas, ed. Princeton, NJ: Princeton University Press, 1998.

opinions, but also, wholeheartedly, to back my heart-felt feelings and my well thought out ideas.

Mary Lee Fraser had studied in Zurich in the 1950s. Her analyst, Mary Briner, not only analyzed her but gave her thorough archetypal training, broadened by institute lectures and classes—a training that Mary Lee handed on to me. However, and what I vastly preferred, was her skill with working on dreams and connecting them to my life. (At the time I first knew her, Mary Lee happened to be lecturing on dreams and active imagination at the Jungian Friends of Jung Group in Eugene.) Mary Lee also loved to reminisce, and I to listen to her stories about her Zurich days and about her fellow students and analysts. I most remember her stories about the women there, and their and her own often-painful struggles. She also related tales of the growing popularity of active imagination and its continued embrace by her fellow enthusiasts especially at the Hotel Sonne in Kusnacht. Many of her stories I later verified when I visited Switzerland, sought out personal interviews, or delved into Harvard's Countway Library of Medicine's archives of personal interviews.[4]

Mary Lee admitted that she rubbed many of the more conventional students and teachers then in Zurich in the wrong way. She rued her awkwardness and lack of tact. (Both attributes I grew to love and trust in spite of the bruises they inflicted.) Her spontaneity and lack of disguise taught me to be less hidden and more honest, at the least, within myself. She was a rangy Texan just under six-feet tall. She rode horses, lived independently, loved women, and spent some of her happiest years near Seattle working with other women as riveters of airplanes during World War II. Her degree in social work and her work with myths and dreams provided an entrée to the Zurich training, but I would imagine she would have been far too outspoken, far too much her own person, and far too prickly, to assume the conventional feminine role required to get her through analytic training in 1950's Switzerland. (Both the San Francisco analysts, Jo Wheelwright and Jane Wheelwright,[5] spent some time in Zurich at the same time she was there; each remember her with affection but also noted how out of place she seemed even among that group of idiosyncratic people.)

---

4 e.g. Douglas, Claire. "The Women Who Helped Found the IAAP." *Newsletter 26*, IAAP 1955–2005, March, 2006.

5 Douglas, Claire. *The Woman in the Mirror: Analytical Psychology and the Feminine.* Boston: Sigo, 1990.

Life seemed to flow back into me along with the joy I felt in bringing my dreams to her each week and in the richness of our work together. It was a richness of spirit and of feeling that not only helped heal me but also inspired me to dig deeper into myself. Her biggest, and most Jungian, gift to me concerned personal responsibility. I found Jung and myself to the extent that I started to learn not to blame outside people or forces, but, instead, to look inside myself. I started to learn to take personal responsibility for what was happening to me, and thus change the way I reacted to things.

I knew, after a few months of work with Mary Lee Fraser, that being a Jungian analyst might be my calling and my path. I could be of use, perhaps, in a more meaningful way. I wanted to help others by cleaning up my own messes. I planned to live in harmony with my surroundings amid the wellsprings of myths, and folk tales, as well as what I'd learned from animal behavior—all enlivened by Jung's lectures and *Collected Works*. Jung's example, and Mary Lee Fraser's probing, engaged all parts of myself and yet seemed to be more inclusive—open to the wonder I was now starting to feel, and continue to feel, in life.

References

The Boston Women's Health Collective. *Our Bodies Ourselves: A Course By and For Women.* Boston: New England Free Press, 1972.

Burns, Robert. *My Heart is in the Highlands.* 1759.

Douglas, Claire. "Christiana Morgan's Visions Reconsidered." (*SFJLJ*, 8, *4,* 1989), 5-27.

————. *The Woman in the Mirror: Analytical Psychology and the Feminine.* Boston: Sigo Press, 1990; Lincoln, NE: Authors Guild BackinPrint.com, 2000.

————. *Translate This Darkness.* Princeton, NJ: Princeton University Press, 1997.

————. "The Women Who Helped Found the IAAP." *Newsletter 26*, IAAP 1955–2005, March, 2006, 167–172.

Douglas, Claire, ed. *The Visions Seminar.* Princeton, NJ: Princeton University Press, 1998.

Jung, C. G. "Paracelsus." *CW 15*, Princeton, NJ: Princeton University Press 1971, 3–12.

————. *The Visions Seminar.* Princeton, NJ: Princeton University Press, 1997.

Morgan, Christiana. *Visions Notebooks, Volume I & III.* Cambridge, MA: Harvard University, Houghton Library, rare books section.

Claire Douglas

Section Two
When Fate Becomes Destiny

If you do not acknowledge your yearning you do not follow yourself.

—The Red Book

A Truchas Story: In the Chimayó Trading and Mercantile, Patricia shows me a wooden carving of Mary becoming a tree. It is so simple, so lovely. She is the Mary of sorrows, deep in prayer. I had told Patricia of a big dream in which I am a woman from long ago, arriving at the Santuario in Chimayó. A priest gives me a brooch in the form of Mary to wear at my throat. I have long puzzled about this dream.

I asked the proprietor if he knew the myth of Mary becoming a tree. "Well, actually," he said, "those aren't leaves, they are the glow of her radiance. But she can be turning into a tree if you want. She is made of a tree, after all."

This Mary has become our "Marked by Fire" goddess. We light a candle to her each morning before we begin our work. N.R.L.

Gilda Frantz: *The Greyhound Path to Individuation*

Jacqueline Gerson: *Finding Meaning: An Unexpected Encounter*

Gilda Frantz and Jacqueline Gerson both have access to the highly imaginative and passionate children they were. They had very different childhoods. Frantz's was chaotic and unprotected. Gerson's childhood in Mexico was warm and loving. But in their essays we can see the luminous and challenging paths of their becoming themselves—the fates they had to suffer, the destinies they claimed.

The Greyhound Path to Individuation

by Gilda Frantz

I have always identified with those Jews whose fate it was during the Holocaust to either have to flee their homeland with what little they could carry, or to be jammed into boxcars and sent off to endure the horror of murders, starvation, and illness in the death camps. As a child born of Jewish parents, I had a frequent fantasy that I could get past Hitler's guards and sneak into his secret hideout and kill him. In my fantasy I didn't know how I would do this, only that somehow a little girl like me might get close enough to Hitler to kill him. I wanted to save my people.

At an earlier time, I worried about the poor of the world and created a solitary game in which I was a scientist who was trying to invent the perfect food that would end starvation throughout the world. It was made of a pinch of cereal and some other types of dry food that I would grind into a powder with a mortar and pestle. In the fantasy play, one pinch of this concoction would end world hunger. I felt very powerful in this fantasy/play, and whenever I was left alone (which was often), I would enter my "laboratory" to grind the cereal into a powdery substance and see in my imagination a starving child being fed just a little of this—and poof!—his or her hunger would cease. In modern Jungian parlance, I felt like an alchemist.

When my mother was in her seventh month of pregnancy with me, on a certain cold winter evening, my parents had an explosive argument, which culminated in my mother's leaving her beautiful home. She woke up my 11-year-old sister and walked out into a stormy, freezing, eastern seaboard night. She obviously expected my father to follow her and bring her back to warmth and safety, but he never did. This event marked both her fate and my sister's and my own fate to wander, gypsy-like, from New York to California.

Jung wrote that as long as children were connected to their parents, they had to suffer the fate of those parents. But when the children grew up and left their parents' home, then they could discover their own destiny. And that is what happened to me.

I grew up feeling that my father was despicable for what he did to my mother, sister, and me by not being there when I was born and seemingly not giving a damn for any of us. His lack of any kind of support forced my mother to be the sole provider for the three of us. As I grew up, I became the conduit mother used as the means to try to get my father to support us. I would call him and ask for money for my mother, but it never worked. We were in the Great Depression and it was almost impossible for my father, a designer of very fine women's millinery, to obtain employment. He didn't support us at all, so my mother had to find ways to put a roof over our heads and food on the table. She worked in so many different jobs: baby nurse, cook in an elementary school cafeteria, cook at a dude ranch, sewing at a WPA factory that made workingmen's clothes. She was a woman of classic, natural beauty and possessed a very lively sense of humor and a wild imagination. She even saw herself as an inventor and, indeed, she invented a lost key service, as well as a way to use the remnants of colored bar soap to make a bubble bath concoction (this was before there was such a thing as bubble bath). Neither of these inventions brought her anything material, although Western Union was interested briefly in the key service, but she enjoyed the creative process involved in their conception and production.

Our instability caused us to move a lot, possibly as often as once every few months. When things were tough and no money was coming in from her jobs, we'd move "just to change our luck," as Mother put it. I went to so many elementary schools I lost count; I never stayed long in any of the schools. We never were hungry, thankfully, as my mother was always able to feed us. She had the gift to make everything seem like an adventure, so life was not bleak growing up, though it was rootless. I said to my analyst once that I'd never had a childhood, but she disagreed and replied, "You had a childhood, you just didn't have the one you would have wanted." And that is the truth.

In the summer of 1938, I was 11 years old and being tossed back and forth, like a potato latke, between my mother in California and my father on the East Coast. My older sister had married the year before, so now there was just my mom and me, which for me was very sad. My mother was still working at whatever job she could find, and I was alone a lot. Also, by that age I was beginning to do what my mother called "develop." My "developing" worried my mother so much that even though we loved one another, she was tossing me back to my father. One morning she told me, "You are going to live with your father, the rat; I can't take care of you anymore."

And then she went on and on about how he never supported us and that the strain and responsibility, now that I was "developing," was just too hard. As I translated her words, *developing* really meant "becoming a woman"—and becoming a woman scared me to death because when I got my period, the first words out of my mother's mouth were an anguished, "Oh, my god, now you are a woman." I wanted to cry because from my vantage point, being a woman was a kind of hell. My mother worried all the time, worked as hard as she could all the time, and as far as I could see, didn't have much of a life. And her breasts hung down to her waist, for which she blamed me. Evidently I nursed her ravenously as an infant, and her pendulous breasts were the result.

I had lived with my father for about 6 months when I was 10½. I was a tall, slender child with long dark-blond hair, large hazel eyes, and a rosy complexion. I looked about 15, but if you heard me talk you would know I was a much younger child. I was intelligent and pretty, but still I was a child. My father didn't know me very well due to my having been raised solely by my mother, but he liked well-mannered pretty children and was proud of me. When I lived with him he made me tell my school chums that my mother was in a sanitarium for her "health." I never knew if he meant a sanitarium for tuberculosis or an insane asylum. Being divorced somehow shamed my dad, and he didn't want the school to know that my parents were divorced.

I missed my mother and got lonesome for my sister and her little girl, so my father eventually sent me back to my mother and now, less than a year later, she was doing something very irrational. Her plan, as she outlined it to me, was to send me by Greyhound bus to New York City, informing my father at the last moment, by Western Union, that I was coming. She said I was leaving the very next morning and she already had a ticket—a child's ticket. This meant I would have to let her bind my little breasts, wear a childish dress, and wear my hair in pigtails so I wouldn't look my age.

I like potato latkes a lot. I love the smell of a latke frying in chicken fat, and I love to hear the sizzling sound the fat makes. With applesauce and sour cream on the side I could eat a lot of latkes, but being like a latke in hot fat didn't appeal to me—in fact, I hated it. As was usual in my life I had no time to say anything to any of my friends, as it was summer and we were all scattered. Because times were so tough, I doubt that many went to summer camp or on vacation, but they did have grandparents who lived on farms or in other towns, and they could visit them and have fun. I had no such luck and was simply reading even more than usual and mostly staying in the room my mom rented with a view of Sunset Boulevard in the Echo Park area.

The next morning my mother put me on a bus, a label pinned on me saying who I was, and we kissed tearfully goodbye. I watched her disappear as the bus pulled away and off we went.

A tired latke child arrived after five days on the road at the station in New York City and saw my father standing there scowling, waiting for the bus door to open. He had on his overcoat and a brown fedora. The wind was blowing, and it was getting cold outside. I was stylishly dressed—though for a younger child—in a coat, hat, and gloves. As I walked down the steps to hug him, he said sternly, "Your mother is crazy. I am married and you cannot live with me." I was always a quiet child not given to tantrums or yelling, but at that moment I wanted to scream. I wanted my mother. Before I knew it, we were walking up the steep stairs to the elevated and waiting for a train. I just went with him; I didn't cry noticeably or make a fuss. Sitting on the train to the Bronx I heard the story. He received the telegram, which came to his home so he had to tell his "new" wife that he had been married before and had a child. (He still didn't tell her about my older sister.) She had a fit and (as my father told the story) pulled at her hair, screaming, "She can't live here! What will my family think of me marrying an older man who had been married before and has a family?" She had married my father after a short courtship, and he had never told her his right age or that he had children, nothing.

I heard only part of what he was saying as I blindly tried to think of a way to escape from him somehow. I felt such hatred and loathing for him, I could hardly look at him. "We're here," he said and took my hand. As the train door closed behind us, I screamed, "My purse, I left it on the seat!" But it was too late, the train was pulling away and my leather handbag and all I had in the world went with it. Then my tears flowed, and I began to feel sorry for myself and for the mess I was in.

We arrived at a house—a huge-looking three-story house on a tree-shaded street. We walked up the stairs to the front door wordlessly. A woman appeared at the door at the sound of the bell and gestured us to come in. The little latke had found a home.

As luck would have it, it turned out to be a real home, and the people were all good people. I actually enjoyed living there after getting over the shock of being unceremoniously dropped into a strange environment. The occupants were Orthodox

German Jews, all Holocaust survivors, and it was at their dinner table that my outrage of what was happening in Germany was ignited. One Sabbath, I sat next to a newly arrived couple, a man and his wife who had escaped from a concentration camp and were now in New York—the tattooed numbers on their arms very visible. They were both very thin, so thin I could see the woman's facial muscles jump and move as she chewed. I listened to them speaking German, and slowly I began to learn German, which was a little like the Yiddish I had learned as a child. Although I had forgotten much of the Yiddish, some of it still came back to me, and in no time I could eavesdrop on conversations to my heart's delight. I learned enough to hate Hitler, and I began having my fantasies of saving the Jews of Germany by killing Hitler.

I stayed in this home happily for about six months. Dutifully I wrote my mother, telling how I missed her, how awful the people were where I lived, but that my father, the rat, didn't care; that he visited me only once a week for about an hour and then gave me a nickel when he left. I told her that I was doing well in school and had made friends, but that she was my beloved mommy and I hoped to see her again. I had not completely forgotten how impulsively she had sent me away on a day's notice, and I knew I was torturing her by telling her how unhappy I was. Well, my clever little plan backfired.

One cold spring morning, the lady of the house awakened me, telling me that my mother was downstairs and that I should dress quickly and come down. I was in shock. Mother, *here*? She had come to "rescue" me from my unhappiness—and off we went to another place, another adventure. Not long after that I wrote to my sister in California and asked her if I could live with her and help her with her baby, who by then was a year old. She gave her consent, so back I went, alone again on the Greyhound bus, this time heading west across the country. My mother stayed in New York. Living with my sister and her little family was a rich experience that gave me the understanding I needed later in life when I became an analyst. In fact, it would be easy to say that my entire early life gave me what I needed in ways that are difficult to write about.

When I was in my early twenties, I met a handsome prince and was carried off into the land of Jung and Jungian analysts. He was older than I, and of a different religion, but neither of those differences mattered because we were both deeply in love. When I learned how old he was, I thought, "Well, I certainly still have a father complex!" I had often dated older men, so being in love with an older man made me realize that

I still had one. I read a lot and was very interested in psychology. (In high school I diagnosed my mother with having delusions of grandeur, which was how I described her to my English teacher.)

After my prince and I became engaged, I began to realize that my future husband had two families, one of his birth and one comprised of Jungian analysts, both colleagues and teachers. Thus, my two sets of in-laws were familial and collegial. Before I met his *family* I met his Jungian analytic friends and teachers. The colleagues looked me over carefully, but I was accepted and hugged and embraced by his birth family. It took me years to feel accepted by the colleagues and for me to accept them, but overnight I loved his birth family and they, me.

I was 23 and the Los Angeles analysts were probably 25 years older than I, or more. I think I dressed the way many young American young women dressed when they were about to meet people important to their betrothed. However, my youthful and stylish presentation stood out rather blatantly amid the conservative, sturdy gray wool suits the analysts and their wives wore. The founders of the Los Angeles Jungian community were all refugees of Hitler's plan to murder millions of Jews. They wore what they brought from Europe and had the look of the intellectuals I had met as a child when my mother went to communist meetings and brought me with her. I observed these intellectuals and found them strange and fascinating. I was 8 or 9 years old. The women let hair grow under their arms and on their legs, and the men didn't shave their beards or cut their hair, so much that they looked scruffy. The analysts didn't look scruffy, however. In fact, there was an elegance to their appearance. They just didn't look like Americans.

As a bride-to-be, I found it ironic that I'd had warm and comfortable feelings for German Jews and other refugees since childhood, but with the refugee analysts I found it particularly hard to feel that I was myself in their company. It was only years later that I learned one of them had actually been in a concentration camp and the others were simply conservative and from another generation, let alone another world. Eventually I did become close with all of them, and loved them, but it took work on all our parts. I know they didn't get behind my persona to see the real me.

My fiancé's way of introducing me to his analytical colleagues and teachers was to bring me to a lecture given by Max Zeller, a kind, gentle soul who spoke with a thick "*ziss und zat*" Berlin accent. I could not understand a word that he said (he had not been in this country that long). On top of that, I had no idea what his topic was about. While I had heard about Freud and knew a little about his theories, Jung was totally a mystery to me. I had never attended such an event before, and I had never before been introduced to a group of people as someone's fiancée. I dressed to the nines for this lecture, wearing a very pretty suit and a tiny hat with a feather, a large feather, that went from the back of the hat and stuck up in front. The hat was a tiny saucer-like shape and the feather was the most outstanding feature. I also wore wrist-length gloves and carried a chic handbag. (Everything matched, as this was 1950.) I thought I looked lovely, but to my shock, I looked so conspicuously overdressed next to the practical outfits worn by the women. In addition, the women all had short, bobbed hair, whereas mine was long and wavy and a golden reddish blond. Not only was I overdressed by everyone else's standards, I also *fell fast asleep* during the talk. Dr. Zeller droned on and on in his thickly accented English, and his words became more and more impossible to understand; against my will sleep overtook me. It was as if Morpheus had intentionally sprinkled sleep dust over my head. I fought sleep, biting my inner cheek and digging my fingernails into my flesh, but it was a losing battle.

Meanwhile, the feather fluttered through the air as my bobbing head betrayed my state. I woke up at the end of the lecture to the sound of polite applause. I quickly gathered my wits to compose myself and shake hands, smiling and nodding, happy to meet all of the people whom my fiancé wanted me to meet.

One woman, the wife of a soon-to-be analyst, tormented me for the next thirty years by telling that story of first meeting me, with that hat with the feather that bobbed as I napped, and how funny it was to her. That she lived a long life is through no doing of mine, because for years I thought I would strangle her each time she told the story to a gathering. Finally, I relaxed and began to see the humor, and just like I am now doing, I too began to tell that story and enjoy the laughter it produced.

One would think with this beginning that I would turn away from Jungian analysis, but I didn't. I went into analysis—with Dr. Zeller! He was a sweet man, and together we dealt with all my adolescent insecurities. After Dr. Zeller, I took time off to have two babies and then was ready for more analysis. I worked with Hilde Kirsch and learned more and more about Jung and how I might, one day, become more conscious. I wrote my dreams down faithfully, did active imagination, drew my dreams, and in general spent a lot of time working on understanding my unconscious and my shadow.

Many, many years later, widowed by then, I was in Zurich on business about the film *Matter of Heart*, which was being shown to the Swiss Jungian community. I met many of Jung's closest followers, and his son Franz Jung, at a party at the Institute after the film was shown.

Since I was to be in Zurich for a week I decided to have what James and Hilde Kirsch had told me about—something known as the *Zurich Experience*. This experience occurred when an American came to Zurich for analysis and stayed for a month, seeing an analyst daily for the entire time, while immersed in dreams, drawings, and writing. I was to be there only a week, but I had something on my mind that might just lend itself to an "instant" analysis. I chose to go to C. A. "Fredy" Meier, who was a brilliant, handsome, virile-looking man. Dr. Meier was puffing on his ever-present pipe when I came to his office. We sat down and were silent for a few moments, giving me a chance to gather my thoughts and take in his office. It was small, cozy, and filled with books and manuscripts he obviously wanted to read, stacked all over the room with beautiful rocks or stones on them to keep them from blowing away.

When he asked why I was in his office, I burst into tears and told him about my terrible inferiority complex around my difficulty with thinking.

"Yah?" he said, reaching into a nearby drawer and handing me a sheaf of papers. "You must take this test, and we will find out about your thinking." And so away I went back to my pension to take a typology test. When I returned a day or two later, Dr. Fredy used a special form to determine my typology by my answers. He puffed on his pipe and then looked at me over the glasses perched on his nose and said, "Gilda, your intuition and feeling are off the chart, maybe one hundred or more, but your thinking and sensation are both three." And looking at me with a delighted look in his eyes, he shouted, "You CAN'T THINK! You shouldn't have a complex since your thinking function is *really* inferior!"

I instantly felt better, and could then move on to some of my dreams. I left Zurich so impressed with this vital man who was so alive and had such a healing effect on me. His last words to me as I went out the door at our last meeting were: "Do research! Jung would have wanted Jungians to do research." And off I went to continue my journey, feeling somehow that I had been initiated into the larger Jungian world with this meeting. Fredy Meier is no longer alive, nor are any of the first-generation analysts. There are now at least three training institutes in Zurich, probably two in Italy, and so on and so forth.

I miss those old days and all those people who became part of my family. My daughter Marlene and son Carl thought of James and Hilde Kirsch as their grandparents, Max and Lore Zeller as their beloved aunt and uncle, and the Zeller children felt like older cousins to them. I too literally grew up in this Jungian environment and found my destiny in their midst.

I am now in my mid-eighties and have been an analyst for almost forty years. The memories I have shared belong to the dusty, distant past, yet they also have a life of their own. My life's journey is a splendid example of luck, love, and individuation, but it is especially one of fulfilling my destiny.

Finding Meaning
An Unexpected Encounter

by Jacqueline Gerson

Childhood is a tender and special stage in an individual's life, a time when playing, discovering, and imagining have an enormous impact on the construction of the sense of self, and my childhood was no exception. From what I remember, I would often wonder about the world I lived in. As a young girl, I constantly challenged what my parents and teachers taught me. Like every child, I looked at old things in new ways. I had my own way of understanding things, of thinking about life, of relating to the world I was getting to know.

Among the many things that I wondered about, there was one that particularly absorbed my attention. I often contemplated the possibility that God would communicate directly with humans in my lifetime, as I heard he had done once upon a time. At school, I was taught the Old Testament stories and learned about the miracles that God had performed on behalf of his chosen people. I was told that he would talk to humans directly, guide them, give them hope. His intervention in human affairs at various moments in history, even though frequently not understood at first, eventually brought meaning to people's lives, and prosperity to those who were lucky enough to be chosen by him. Although he was never actually seen by human eyes, never apprehended in physical form, his voice had been heard, and it had always been clear in those instances that it was his voice speaking. And when he intervened in human affairs, there was never any doubt that it was his hand that was at work. His presence was felt, and his will was made known.

Difficult though it was to believe what my teachers were teaching me, I came to accept it as true. However, deep down in my innermost thoughts, even as a little girl, I wondered: How could we be so sure that it was God—God speaking, God acting, God leading? I wanted to experience for myself what I was being taught. I dared to question the unquestionable, to doubt what we were forbidden to doubt, even as I yearned to believe it.

I was told that whenever God's chosen people had faced difficulties in ancient times, he would intervene to make the difficulties go away. Well, I had problems too, and I hoped that God would do something to make them go away. One particular issue that I was struggling with at that time in my life was that I wanted to be a dancer, to devote all my time to dancing, instead of having to go to school. When I danced, I was able to experience my body in relation to space. I would feel my arms, my legs, my entire being blending into the music. My body was its own master. Dancing led me to discover a very important source of wisdom and pleasure: my own physical body. Dancing was private, intimate, my direct experience, and I had no doubts about what I was experiencing. Unlike the intellectual material that I was learning in school, which raised more questions than it provided answers for and therefore left me feeling unsatisfied, dancing brought peace to my mind and nourishment to my soul.

So at night, when I went to bed and said my night prayers, thanking God for the life he had given me, as I was taught to do, I would also ask him to help me with this problem. I would pray that he would make my parents understand how important dance was in my life. But it seemed that God did not hear my prayers, or if he did, he chose not to answer them. I begged him to convince my parents to allow me to make dancing my life's work, but instead of having my petition granted, I still had to attend school every day and listen to stories about God performing miracles for other people while he ignored me.

Schoolwork seemed to go on for years and years. The miracle I had hoped for did not happen. As I grew older and entered adolescence, my thought processes began to change along with my body. My very basic childhood questions about the transcendental evolved as I did, taking on at this stage in my life a more demanding and challenging tone of voice toward the adult world. Even as I was forced to memorize and recite passages from the Bible, I would ask questions such as: How could the Old Testament patriarchs be so sure that it was God who was speaking to them? On what basis did they dare to claim that God was speaking through them and expressing his will for the rest of humanity?

From being the youngest in my family, and being told constantly what I was supposed to do, even which school to go to, and what to believe in, I suddenly found myself with a will of my own and the ability to challenge the establishment. But under the surface of my rebellious attitude toward authority, my old question remained alive. I kept wondering: In case God continued in the miracle business (as generation after generation of ancients had insisted he did, and as my own family, academic authorities, and the most recent authors on the subject were still predicting he would), would I be able to recognize his hand in the miracles? If he spoke to me directly, remote as that possibility was, how would I recognize that it was his voice? And would I even be able to hear it?

After completing high school, I studied at the Music Conservatory, became a Montessori guide, and earned a college degree. All the while, I continued to dance on the side. Even though I never got a degree in dance, my passion for dancing remained alive. It was only when I was in my early thirties, when I was working with movement awareness and music, that I discovered Jungian psychology.

My initial encounter with Jung came through casual participation in a dream interpretation workshop. For me, dreams could be seen as spontaneous choreographies created by the psyche, and like dance, they were full of meaning.

It was out of a desire to deepen our understanding of the Jungian approach to the image and the psyche that a few like-minded friends and I formed a study group. At that time, Jungian literature was not available in Mexico. Jung himself was virtually unknown. I remember having to go to the United States to get books by or about Jung, bring them back to Mexico, photocopy the newly acquired treasure and circulate it among the study group members, and even translate the difficult parts into Spanish so as to be able to share and understand these very new ideas, which we all found deeply enlightening. We discovered that Jungian psychology was not only difficult to understand because of its daring and innovative approach to the psyche, but also very different from the prevailing view in the field of psychology in Mexico at that time. Unfortunately, there was no one in Mexico knowledgeable enough in Jungian thought to guide us in our understanding of this revolutionary thinker, and so we had to stumble along on our own, sorting out whatever we could to the best of our ability.

Among the many ideas to which Jungian psychology opened my mind, there was one in particular that captured my heart, one for which all that effort seemed eminently worthwhile. It was the possibility of bringing together body and mind. I saw that dance and academic studies need not be separate and opposed disciplines. There seemed to be a space in Jungian thought where the two could come together and co-exist in perfect harmony. Dance need no longer be merely an after-school or after-work activity, a hobby, as had previously been supposed. It could even be an important means through which the psyche could express itself, an important source of wisdom, which I had already tapped into as a child. I had finally found a theoretical framework for what, until then, had been only empirical; in Jung I had found a resonance with the sentiments I had expressed secretly through dance, as well as an implicit acknowledgement of the importance of dance, its transcendent quality, and its potential for transforming people's lives. Jungian psychology provided a space for and a way of valuing and giving recognition to what I had been feeling in the quiet solitude of my inner self for so many years.

I began reading about Jung's daring proposition regarding the existence of a collective unconscious, about archetypes, and so on. For the first time, I encountered such terms as "shadow" and "anima" and "animus." But beyond these important concepts, the possibility of putting together what for years had been forced to remain apart in my life—body and mind—gave me a sense of wholeness, of a coming together of what had once seemed irreconcilable.

This small group of pioneers in Jungian psychology in Mexico represented for me the container, the cocoon in which my new identity was coming to life. But unfortunately, it did not last long enough to deliver on its initial promise. All sorts of exigencies contrived to swallow up the beam of light that was just beginning to enlighten our lives. The group's dissolution left my friends and me in an even darker space than the one in which we were when we began. The situation felt really hopeless.

Not being able to continue exploring this newly found approach to body and mind was a major setback for me. With my group dissolving, I felt alone and disoriented. I had no idea how to proceed, or whether I even wanted to go on. It was a time of great upheaval in my life.

Around that time, my mother, who was still relatively young, suddenly died. My outlook on life became so dark that I even forgot my childhood questions about God's existence and miracles. As so often happens to adults, one can get so caught up in dealing with the trivialities of everyday life that one forgets the really important things. One can easily lose contact with the inner child, even as it continues to wonder unheeded in the background. I became one of those adults: I lost contact.

In an attempt to recover from the great losses that had piled up on me almost simultaneously, I went to visit one of the main bookstores in a beautiful old colonial section of Mexico City: Coyoacán. Browsing through books in a bookstore or library has been, and still is, one of my favorite pastimes. As I walked through the bookstore, nothing in particular caught my attention. Even though it was a really big bookstore, and I usually left it not just with more books than I intended to buy, but with many more than I was actually able to read, this particular time I could not find a single thing that I cared about. Finally, tired of looking for something that would grab my attention, I left. For the first time in my life, I found myself with empty hands and an empty mind, but worst of all, an empty heart.

I took a walk around the plaza and finally sat down in one of the many coffee shops outside the bookstore. As I sipped absently at my cappuccino, I began to think about what was going on inside me. I just could not believe that I had reached the point where I was unable to find even a single book that would interest me! I thought I might be getting sick. After sitting and drinking my cappuccino for a while, I decided to go back into the bookstore. The thought that there was nothing I could find that was appealing enough to read was simply unbearable.

I went back into the bookstore not knowing exactly what I expected to happen that would be different this time, and there it was! On one of the tables off to one side near the entrance was displayed a new book that had just arrived. The book was *Memorias, Sueños y Pensamientos* por C.G. Jung (*Memories, Dreams, Reflections* by C.G. Jung). Almost reverently, I picked up one of the copies on display. There, in my favorite bookstore, in my language, in my country, in my hands—finally a book by Jung! I started to cry. I could still cry!

I opened the book in my hands, but I could not read a thing since my eyes were full of tears. But who needed to read or understand just then, when what I needed to bring me back to life, to help me find my own path, had been so clearly revealed in such an unexpected manner? I left the bookstore hugging my book to my chest. I needed to walk, to move, to dance. And I haven't stopped dancing since that fateful day. Dancing with my memories, my dreams, and my reflections. Dancing life.

In a country where even today (twenty years later) there is no Jungian institute, I found a way to do what needed to be done to become a certified Jungian analyst. The energy, the endurance, the courage to do so came from that experience at the bookstore, which remains alive in my memory even as I write this.

Having started out on the long path to becoming a Jungian analyst, I began to develop a familiarity with many of the fascinating and thought-provoking ideas that Jung proposed. Among them, there was one in particular that gave me an understanding of what I had experience that morning in my favorite bookstore and changed my life. Jung even provided me with a word for it. I found out that Jung had studied these seemingly chance encounters extensively and had given them the name "synchronicity."

In "On Synchronicity," Jung wrote:

> As its etymology shows, this term has something to do with time or, to be more accurate, with a kind of simultaneity. Instead of simultaneity we could also use the concept of *meaningful coincidence* of two or more events, where something other than the probability of chance is involved.[1]

Finding the first of Jung's books to be translated into Spanish, and especially finding it seemingly by chance on my return to that bookstore, had such an impact on me because it came at exactly that time in my life when I needed something to pick me up out of the pit I had sunk into. The coincidence was far too precise to be the result of random forces. Finding that book was like finding a long-lost loved one and suddenly realizing the possibility of re-establishing the soul-nourishing relationship one once had with that person. Even though I was blessed with a loving family, and have been for most of my life, I had ended up personally and professionally in a dark alley. In a life that had lost its meaning, its purpose, and its direction, that book appeared, seemingly out of nowhere, as a beacon of light to guide me out of my darkness.

As I think back, I realize that had a similar incident occurred in the life of someone else, or even at a different point in my own life, it would not have had the impact it did, and it might not have taken on the aspect of a turning point as it did for me at that time. From my reading of Jung, I learned that synchronistic events bring the objective and subjective worlds together in some meaningful way. In my case, the event in the objective world was Jung's book being translated into Spanish and released in Mexico at that specific time. In my subjective world, I was going through a crisis that needed immediate resolution. These two worlds converged and intersected when I made that fateful decision to go back into the bookstore at almost the very moment when the

---

1 C. G. Jung, *CW* 8 , ¶ 969.

newly arrived book was put on display. That coincidence gave rise to an encounter between the inner and the outer that I experienced as profoundly meaningful.

According to Jung, what makes synchronistic events so striking, and therefore so meaningful, is their numinous quality. Those who experience such an event get the feeling they are in the presence of something beyond ordinary human understanding, something that might be called "God." For me, the experience in the bookstore had a distinctly numinous—almost miraculous—quality to it. It was a definite turning point in my life. Not only did it inspire me to begin formal training to become a Jungian analyst, but it also reawakened the inner child within me, and with it the capacity for wonderment and curiosity, and the eternal quest to find an answer to that ever-vexing question about God performing miracles. I always knew God does not manifest himself directly to our sight, but finds ways to make his voice heard. I think I heard God's voice, and experienced one of his miracles, when I found that book in that bookstore on that fateful afternoon. I could feel his presence guiding me. Hope returned to my life, and I got moving once again, writing letters, looking for possibilities, making contact with people in other parts of the world who had themselves had a similar encounter with Jung's work. I found myself an analyst, and supervisors, and tutors, who guided me in buying books, reading, and studying. But above all, my life-changing synchronistic experience got me back into dancing—dancing not on a theatrical stage, but on the grand stage of life, dancing in the world, dancing life itself.

Jung emphasized that synchronistic events are unintentional and acausal. We have no part to play in their occurrence. The only direct and purposeful participation that we might have in them is in responding to them as to a call. The narrowness of personal planning, of purely ego-oriented desires, has no part to play in the miracle of synchronicity. When I was a child, I wanted to dance all day long instead of going to school, knowing that my parents would never allow it. That is the miracle I begged God to perform. Now I don't need to literally dance all day long, as I once dreamed of doing. I have found out what the true essence of dancing is: it is the capacity to move in life; to discover one's own rhythm in everything one does; to step in time with the rhythm of life; to know when to go forward and when to stop, when to gather energy and leap, and when to hold back; to live gracefully and elegantly, embodying beauty and an esthetic of congruence; to celebrate the possibility of expressing oneself, of giving form to one's interpretation of life's choreography, of releasing one's uniqueness, a possibility inherent in every movement that we make, throughout our life. This is how I find myself nowadays, dancing and observing other people dance, every day of my life.

It is not difficult to see how unusual accidental occurrences can have meaning for the individual who is trying to figure out what dance means, or is traveling miles to attend analysis in a language that is not his or her own. All of us who have, at some time in our life, experienced synchronicity in action share the unmistakably recognition that it changed our life.

Allow me to introduce you to a fascinating paper entitled "Reflections on 'Chance', 'Fate', and Synchronicity," written in 1989 by Dr. Gerhard Adler. In that "highly personal" contribution, as he himself describes it, Adler writes: "As a young man I was very fond of dancing; I was particularly fond of fancy dressballs [*sic*] as they were *en vogue* in the Berlin of the twenties and early thirties."[2] He goes on to describe, in close detail, how one particular Sunday back in 1928, when he was exhausted from having danced for two consecutive nights with hardly any sleep, he was invited by a friend to a party. At first he declined, but eventually he yielded to the pressure of his friend's insistence. At the party, his friend introduced him to a woman coincidentally named Mrs. Adler, an acquaintance of Jung's. That chance encounter at the party developed into a friendship, in which Mrs. Adler took on the role of Dr. Adler's "anima-lady." She stimulated his curiosity in Jung's ideas and eventually convinced him to go into Jungian analysis. At that time in his life, he was, by his own admission, "a fairly confused young man" who had "not really found my professional way of life at all."[3] Adler goes on to recount how he ended up in analysis with Jung himself, and then asks:

> This is how my analytical career started ... but what is this *this*? What role did my namesake anima play in it? ... Would I ever have had this chance of working personally with Jung without having arrived reluctantly and tired at this particular Sunday afternoon party?[4]

He concludes: "I cannot help feel that some divine intervention had arranged it all."[5] Commenting on his meeting with Mrs. Adler, he writes:

---

2 Gerhard Adler, "Reflections on 'Chance,' 'Fate,' and Synchronicity," *Psychological Perspectives* 20, no. 1 (1989): 20.

3 Adler, "Reflections."

4 Adler, "Reflections," 22.

5 Adler, "Reflections."

[t]he fate of two people was deeply intertwined in a complex pattern due to what in ordinary language one can only call a 'chance-meeting' ... a 'meaningful coincidence' of inner fate and external events.[6]

Adler then makes the all-important connection: "Such a meaningful coincidence is, of course, a striking example of synchronicity."[7] Speaking of synchronistic events in general, he says that they are "rare moments when the meeting of two fates produces a miraculous illumination, when the veil is lifted and two destinies become visible in their interdependence."[8]

In Adler's account of his initial meeting with his "namesake anima" and the events that followed, I was particularly struck by his admission that he could not help feeling that "some divine intervention had arranged it all." My childhood question about God's existence and miracles was answered once again, and in a somewhat synchronistic manner as well, for out of the vast body of Jungian literature, I just happened to find this particular paper by Gerhard Adler, who, like me, both loved to dance and through "some divine intervention" came to love Jungian psychology and dedicate his life to it.

In the course of my reading, I came across another author whose work resonated with me: Robert H. Hopcke. He does research into synchronicity as a psychic phenomenon as it is manifested in various aspects of our daily life. His book *There Are No Accidents: Synchronicity and the Stories of Our Lives* is a compilation of real-life experiences of ordinary people that illustrate this Jungian concept. Particularly relevant to my own experience is the association he makes between synchronicity and emotions. In a section entitled "Think, Don't Feel: Synchronicity and the Modern Distrust of Emotional Reality," he writes:

Jung noted that the events we call synchronistic have a certain unmistakable emotional tone to them which he called "numinous," borrowing the term from theologian Rudolph Otto. Numinosity is that experience we have when we feel that we are undeniably, irresistibly, and unforgettably in the presence of the Divine, our experience of something which transcends our human limitations. This heightened qual-

---

6 Adler, "Reflections."
7 Adler, "Reflections," 23.
8 Adler, "Reflections," 30.

ity of feeling which accompanies synchronistic events is perhaps the most striking characteristic of such events.[9]

When I first read Hopcke's words, they reminded me of my own childhood and adolescent doubts with regard to the Old Testament accounts of God's miracles, or perhaps my wanting to be like the many people in the course of history who had been fortunate enough to experience God's miraculous intervention. I had wondered if I would be able to recognize it, if and when it happened to me. Hopcke's book made me realize that in the presence of the Divine there can be no doubts. I read his fascinating accounts of the synchronistic experiences of numerous people and the life-changing effect these experiences had on them, only this time, instead of feeling skeptical, I felt a sense of solidarity, of belonging to the human race, the only species that is privileged to experience the Divine and know it for certain.

As a child I wondered about God performing miracles, but in my nearsightedness I was unable to see the miracles I was taught about were not at all what people were expecting. In fact, they were beyond anything people could ever have imagined! Miracles are so far removed from our everyday experience (and that is perhaps precisely what makes them miracles) they are incomprehensible to our understanding and independent of our will. Hopcke writes:

> Jung's view of the purposive nature of psychological phenomena undergirds his concept of synchronicity. In chance events both emotionally and symbolically meaningful, our psychological experience of a synchronicity always occurs to enable us to move forward in some way. This is why synchronicities happen at those all-important points of transition in our lives. Much like the external, social help we often seek out during such periods, the psyche sometimes provides, in the form of meaningful coincidences, a form of internal and psychological help.[10]

In my particular case, I had no specific expectations. I could not have been looking for something that I was unable even to dream about as being within the realm of possibility. The truth of the matter for me, as well as for Adler, was that we were both disoriented and stuck, with no clear path ahead of us. We needed help, and the synchronistic experience provided it, making it possible for us to move forward in

---

9 Robert H. Hopcke, *There Are No Accidents: Synchronicity and the Stories of Our Lives* (New York: Riverhead Books, 1997), 30.
10 Robert H. Hopcke, *There Are No Accidents*, 42.

life. That help came in the form of an encounter with the Divine, in us and around us. The Divine is not an external figure, as most children (and many adults) think. To encounter the Divine is to discover that the psyche "sometimes provides, in the form of meaningful coincidences, a form of internal and psychological help." In summing up what he calls "Jung's metapsychology," Adler writes: "It is the unique experience of the miracle and enigma of the psyche, in the face of which awe and reverence are the only possible answers."[11]

As I write this paper, I have that feeling of awe and reverence once again, as I recall a very old and almost-forgotten memory. When I was five years old I fell seriously ill. The symptoms of my illness scared me to death. Not only did they feel frightening, but the medical uncertainty surrounding my diagnosis made them appear even scarier. I picked that up from the caregivers around me and was myself very afraid. I remember one day, when my fear seemed stronger than I could bear, telling my mother, with the deepest sincerity, that when I grew up I wanted to be a doctor, not like the ones who gave medicines and injections, since they didn't do any good, but one who would help children not to feel afraid. I can still remember crying and almost confessing, with my limited childish vocabulary, that I wanted to be a psychotherapist. I asked my mother if it was clear to her what I was trying to clarify for myself: wanting to make children feel good, as I so desperately wanted for myself. My mother understood, and I felt embraced. I believe it was then, in that state of feeling so wounded myself, that I had my first glimpse of the possibility of becoming the wounded healer I eventually turned out to be.

As the years passed, I forgot this incident, since soon after I recovered from my illness, I discovered dance. For me, dance was deeply psychologically healing. It made me feel engaged in the pleasure of being alive. I felt once again the sense of well-being that I had lost for a while. I discovered movement, and through my body I was able to establish contact with myself. This made me stronger and happier. But it also generated in me the desire to dance all day, and that in turn led me to aspire to become a dancer, and I forgot all about my early ambition to be a psychotherapist.

This memory, long buried and only now, as I write, brought to consciousness, carries with it the realization that my vocation to be a healer arose at a very early age, as is often the case, out of my own personal history. I wanted to help children, everyone in fact, not to be afraid, to feel a sense of well-being in their bodies, in themselves,

---

11 Adler, "Reflections," 32.

in their lives. For me, personally, dance was and still is the *via regia* to achieving that goal.

But I have also discovered that while dance is an important means of achieving well-being in my life, it is not necessarily so for everyone. In fact, there are all kinds of possibilities on the individual's path to healing, depending on his or her unique manner of being in the world and his or her particular life experiences. The ultimate goal is the healing of a suffering and needy soul. That is really what gives meaning to my life, and what I dedicated my life to doing. But, perhaps, none of it would have been possible without that unexpected encounter with the numinous that afternoon in my favorite bookstore.

I feel fortunate to be able to do the work that I do, privileged to be a Jungian analyst in a country where it is difficult to be one. But even further, I feel extremely gratified for having felt God's presence in my life. Writing this paper has been yet another instance of making contact with the Divine, as parts of myself were revealed to me as I wrote, adding deeper meaning to my work, my dance, and my life.

References

Adler, Gerhard. "Reflections on 'Chance,' 'Fate,' and Synchronicity." *Psychological Perspectives*, 20, no. 1 (1989): 16–33.

Hopcke, H. Robert. *There Are No Accidents: Synchronicity and the Stories of Our Lives.* New York: Riverhead Books, 1997.

Jung, C.G. *The Collected Works of C.G. Jung.* Vol. 8. Princeton: Princeton University Press, 1960.

Section Three
Winter Road

Life is a journey and you choose to be a pilgrim or a tourist.

Brochure for El Santuario de Chimayó

A Truchas story: I must have been in my late twenties when I saw an exhibit of Georgia O'Keefe's life work. I have always remembered the last painting, Winter Road. It is a curved stroke of black on white. It seemed so eloquent to me, speaking to the long road of a life, and how clear a shape it can take when fully and creatively lived. I hoped to live such a life.

That image sprang to my mind's eye this morning when Patricia and I sat and meditated. I saw it as a glyph for the stories in this collection— telling of a life pilgrimage. Later at brunch at the home of Trish and Leonardo, we were enchanted by the dining room chairs. Leonardo had crafted a set of painted and accessorized chairs whose backs were the faces and bodies of iconic women: Marilyn, Frida, Georgia. I got to sit on Georgia's lap. N.R.L.

Jean Kirsch: *The I Ching and I: Reflections on a Jungian Individuation*

Chie Lee: *Old Roots, New Soil*

Jean Kirsch and Chie Lee tell stories of their pilgrimages that take us to China, although in very different ways. Kirsch finds guidance and fatherly mentoring in the ancient Chinese book of divination, the *I Ching*. Lee came from a difficult history in China to find her way to Los Angeles, and to Jung.

The *I Ching* and I
Reflections on a Jungian Individuation

by Jean Kirsch

Jung began his foreword to the 1950 Bollingen edition of the *I Ching* thus:

> [s]ince I am not a sinologue, a foreword to the Book of Changes from my hand must be a testimonial of my individual experience with this great and singular book.[1]

I would like to echo his statement, adding that I have never made this great and singular book a subject of intellectual study. Rather, it has been my constant companion and ever-helpful guide for over forty years. Only recently has it taken human form among the characters that people my inner landscape. It came about because of a dream.

> I dreamed I had the middle seat on a flight to the east coast, and as we prepared for landing a conversation sprang up with the gentleman seated on my left. He was Chinese, a handsome, trim man of about fifty with hair graying at the temples. He wore a dark suit and modest tie. In heavily accented, somewhat formal English, he introduced himself as Doctor Li, a general physician from Central China. He was en route to the funeral of his paternal uncle, making the trip to represent the large extended family his uncle had left behind when he emigrated in the late 1960s. This was his first visit to the USA. As we talked I had the feeling that I had known this man for a very long time. He was familiar and trustworthy. I felt I had met a soul-mate.

As I lay in bed that morning, contemplating the dream, I linked the modest and direct man, Dr. Li, with the *I Ching* and since then, to use the *I Ching* has been, for me, "to consult Dr. Li." To understand the role he has played in my life, you need to know a little about my story, with special emphasis on re-collections[2] since my own "emigration" in the late 1960s to the new world of Jungian psychology.

---

1 C.G. Jung, "Foreword," in *The* I Ching *or Book of Changes*, (Princeton University Press, 1950/1967), *xxi.*

2 I use the word as in "re-collection of projections," as Marie Louis von Franz used the term in her book, *Projection and Re-collection in Jungian Psychology: Reflections of the Soul.*

I was born toward the end of the Great Depression, and my indifferent father soon abandoned his immature young wife, me, and my little brother. In my mind's eye is the enduring image of him in a gray overcoat and fedora, walking up the lane to the road and never looking back, leaving me behind with my furious and heartbroken mother. His departure produced in me a great absence. Where Father should have been was a gaping hole—a father-hole, as one friend named it for me. Its effect has been to impede my relationship to the outer world.

When I feel my way back into my childhood, I recall yearning for life's experience. Money was in short supply, as were education and culture. Our home in the Ohio countryside offered few opportunities, and I chafed against its limits, although I was keenly receptive to the numinous in nature. Perhaps even then I had a vague glimmering of the varied and intense life that would unfold before me, and I was impatient for it! I couldn't wait to start school, but I discovered Sunday school at the little church down the road and badgered to be taken. My mother was depressed and angered by the censure she felt as a divorced woman, and although she behaved responsibly, she did it without grace. It was simply a negating and barren way to grow up—socially, intellectually, and emotionally. Still, my mother modeled two great gifts that have served me all of my life: a capacity for steady, hard work and, strangely enough, a genuine appreciation for classical music.

I will skip rapidly over vast tracts of my life to focus on the *I Ching* and how it became for me a "good enough father." But before I go into that story, I want to say a few words about the absence of the father in feminine development. The masculine side of the psyche of an un-fathered woman tends to lack grounding in reality, both inner and outer. She may radiate confidence and give the appearance of competence, she may even become competent, but her relationship to outer reality lacks connection to a basic sense of self-trust. A man relating to such a woman might never feel quite sure that he is taken for who he is and is often astonished by the gaps in her confidence and judgment. She may come across as one version of what they used to call in the olden days "an anima woman." I believe this derives from an unconscious sense of her father's absence; thus, she looks outward to find the masculine principle and dynamism she lacks within. This version is a mirror image of the anima woman who was daddy's favorite.

In my case, no-father turned out favorably, for it gave me a chance to create his ideal and go in search of him. For the most part, I chose good models and constructed an internal masculine image largely through fantasy, projection, and re-collection—although desire, hard work, and a good mind helped considerably to make him a functioning psychic reality. Framed within a Jungian context, I could define it in terms of animus development and make it an aspect of Self that I might amend through the individuation process. As my accomplishments brought me into intimate contact with groups of highly successful and competent people, I became more keenly aware of something missing inside. With the help of the *I Ching*, I began a new construction project in the potential space left empty where father should have been, working on what had been "spoiled by the father" to develop ethical principles and relational attitudes. Simultaneously, the metaphoric language of the *I Ching* stimulated my pragmatic, sensation-trained mind to grow wings, while it grounded my overactive fantasy life.

My journey from a farmhouse on the Western Reserve Road in Ohio to a suburban street in Palo Alto, California, is a long chapter, so I must race you through the decades. Skipping over childhood and adolescence, I first went to nursing school, and after graduating, traveled north, where I studied at the University of Alaska, eventually earning a BS degree, while on long summer days and in winter on weekends I worked as a flight attendant for Wein Alaska Airlines, which served as a lifeline for arctic Alaska. I landed at Stanford Medical School, intending to become a surgeon, until I met and fell in love with Tom. One thing led to another, bringing me here, to the present—a grandmother and aging Jungian analyst, writing this memoir. Years of analysis and positive life experience—especially my relationship with my husband Tom, and the family and friends that have surrounded us—have modified the effects of an internalized negative mother, but the father-hole was a different matter. Modest academic achievement, some professional competence, and the general respect of my colleagues have been the rewards of good luck, good health, and lots of hard work. Yet, I still needed a presence with wisdom and a breadth of vision over human experience to help clarify my thinking in the face of confusing information and guide me along paths that added to the general well-being. In the absence of father the *I Ching* became that presence.

Early in our courtship, Tom introduced me to the *I Ching*. I had met him on my psychiatry rotation at Stanford. He was a clinical supervisor to the resident to whom I'd been assigned as a medical student. Recently separated, he was on the lookout, so within weeks we were dating. He had just made a tour of Alaska with a National

Institute of Mental Health team, sent to evaluate the mental health needs of the state. His fresh and vivid impressions of Alaska were the source of his lively projections, which fell onto me. From my side, some dark impulse toward individuation had been brewing deep within, and it resonated with what was most active in Tom. He was a candidate at the C.G. Jung Institute of San Francisco—which meant nothing to me—but he was passionate about it, and that spoke to me, and I became curious. Instinctively, I trusted him. Our shared myth, though, has been that marriage came about because of the *I Ching*.

We had been dating for two months when I browsed his bookshelves out of curiosity and came upon the *I Ching*. "What's this?" I asked innocently. He patiently explained that it was an ancient Chinese book of divination that one might consult for advice about an issue of great importance, when one could not see one's way forward. "Huh," I said, "could we try it?"

"Yes, but you first have to ask a question."

Playfully, I asked, "So, where is this relationship going?"

To my surprise, he took me utterly seriously and carefully instructed me about throwing the three coins in the proper order, tallying their values, and finding the corresponding hexagram. What happened next is an apocryphal story. I came up with the Hexagram of Marriage, with no changing lines. Tom's mind was blown! I felt destiny's call!

Well, if you know the *I Ching*, you will recognize our error: no hexagram in the Bollingen translation represents the archetype of marriage. Tom recalls it was a single digit hexagram, so we concluded it was Hexagram 8: Holding Together. However, as I told you at the beginning, I am no scholar of the *I Ching*. I had taken Jung at his word when he wrote in the foreword:

> The *I Ching* insists upon self-knowledge throughout. The method by which this is to be achieved is open to every kind of misuse, and therefore is not for the frivolous-minded and immature; nor is it for intellectuals and rationalists. It is appropriate only for thoughtful and reflective people who like to think about what they do and what happens to them.[3]

---

3 Jung, "Foreword," *xxxiii.*

And so I have never studied it systematically, nor memorized its contents. My goal has not been to develop expertise, but to read it deeply within the context of a living situation. This makes each consultation an approach to an as-yet-unknown Other, whose response I seek with an open mind.

Tom and I have maintained the story, unchallenged, for over four decades that my first *I Ching* consultation produced the Hexagram of Marriage! Tom's and my backgrounds were worlds apart, and bringing our two cultures into union was challenging. Tom is the son of German Jews in exile. He was born in London, and during the Battle of Britain his family left for the United States. After an imperiled voyage across the North Atlantic, they arrived safely on Ellis Island and traveled on to sunny Los Angeles, where his parents began practicing and teaching Jung's psychology. From childhood Tom had been steeped in Jungian lore and European culture. Reed College and Yale Medical School had grounded him academically, and he was an advanced candidate on the verge of analytic certification when we met.

My introduction to Tom's world became a baptism in fire, considering my background and ambitions at the time of our meeting in 1967. I had entered Stanford with the goal of becoming a surgeon, and I had completed several elective clerkships in that field. In the thick and thin that has been our marriage, the powerful symbol of that early *I Ching* has served as a talisman, proof that our union has profound meaning in the greater scheme of the Self. Through this most difficult of spiritual pathways, the *I Ching* has been like a good-enough father, reminding me always of my higher self and teaching me to take the long view, to learn to bear whatever strong emotion threatened to tear us apart at the moment.

My introduction to Jung and analytical psychology, on the other hand, was a baptism in mud! I nearly drowned in *prima materia,* the dark shadow stuff that alchemy transforms, before I found my footing. (A dream early in my analysis saw me trying to outrun a landslide during an earthquake, hand in hand with a little girl. From the sky a booming voice said, "Mud is safe!") At first I was just trying to build new ego structures from which to relate to the Self. I was overwhelmed by its affects, and although I could appreciate the wonderful potential in its imagery, I had trouble making them useful for my life.

Also, discovering a therapeutic method in Jung's Collected Works is a patchwork process at best. Dr. Li helped me to build creative bridges between my ego and the affects and the images that emerged from the archetypal unconscious. To frame a question for the *I Ching*, I had to focus my attention on my actual experience and was forced to find words for my unclear perceptions and inchoate affects; this was a helpful discipline in itself. Reliably, the *I Ching* came up with a surprisingly on-the-mark hexagram each time. I then had to translate back into personal terms the images and metaphoric language of the hexagram. The situation I faced and my inner experience came into greater accord as they were amplified and re-framed by this dialogical process. My perceptions shifted. I gained a sense of direction and purpose and could imagine myself creatively responding to the situation. Hand in hand with my dreams, personal analysis, sandplay, analytic training, and clinical experience, I slowly developed the ability to read Dr. Li's dreamlike utterances. A symbolic attitude began to take shape in my psyche. I discovered my ability to read the meaningful symbolic language of my patients' dreams, with the help of their associations. I was developing narrative competence.

Early in my use of the *I Ching*, I developed my own method of approaching it. My first principle was to respect it. Hexagram 4: Youthful Folly[4] taught me not to importune, not to ask twice about the same issue, unless encouraged by it to do so. I viewed the book as I would a dignified sage who would never allow me to regard him lightly. My second principle grew out of this relationship of respect: I prepared myself for each approach by setting aside enough time to write as much as I was able to bring forth pertaining to the issue at hand. If I had made a decision already and needed the *I Ching's* perspective on its likely consequences, I would say so. Only then would I open the book and throw the three coins onto its front page, six times in succession, and record the numbers for the six lines.

How does it work? Jung offers the hypothesis that the *I Ching* works through the principle of synchronicity, which assumes that the essential quality of two distinct moments—there and then, and here and now—are alike in meaningful ways.

[W]hoever invented the *I Ching* was convinced that the hexagram worked out in a certain moment coincided with the latter in quality no less than in time. To him, the hexagram was the exponent of the moment in which it was cast [and he] … takes the coincidence of events in space and time as meaning something more than mere

---

4 *The* I Ching *or Book of Changes*, 20.

chance, namely, a peculiar interdependence of objective events among themselves as well as with the subjective (psychic) states of the observer or observers.[5]

I believe Jung offers us a key to his own use of the *I Ching* in this foreword. Following his recommendations, I have found that his method invariably works for me. Thus, a series of Chinese scholars through the centuries worked out a system of 64 essential and typical situations; by adding the variables of changing and unchanging lines, of primary and secondary trigrams, and elaborating them in a metaphoric language, they created a document which allows for innumerable ways in which the typical situation might be embodied by a future questioner in any given moment.

It is not easy to grasp the underlying logic. Yet my repeated experience convinces me that at the moment of throwing the coins, my situation corresponds to one that was described over two thousand years ago, in form, if not in content. I am convinced that what we call chance is influenced by this remarkable underlying correspondence, which will bring the two moments into alignment, provided that the moment is sufficiently charged with meaning to constellate the correspondence and the questioner's intent is heartfelt. This is what makes the *I Ching* a text with eternally living meaning. As Jung writes, "These powers form, as it were, the living soul of the book. As the latter is thus a sort of animated being, the tradition assumes that one can put questions to the *I Ching* and expect to receive intelligent answers."[6] Constructed as a practical resource to help people manage the inevitable chaos and change that is inherent in all life forms, it is still a resource, for human nature does not change in fundamental ways.

An example will suggest the kinds of experience I have had which stand behind my acceptance and will illustrate how I interpret my reading in the moment. In 1996, before I began my term of office as president of the C.G. Jung Institute of San Francisco, I discussed the matter with the *I Ching*, expressing my anxieties and hopes. Hexagram 53: Development, or Gradual Progress[7] was its response, with only one changing line, Six in the fourth place, which reads:

> The wild goose gradually draws near the tree.
>
> Perhaps it will find a flat branch. No blame.

---

5 Jung, "Foreword," *xxiv.*
6 Jung, "Foreword," *xxv-xxvi.*
7 *The* I Ching *or Book of Changes*, 204.

"A tree is not the suitable place for a wild goose. But if it is clever, it will find a flat branch on which it can get a footing. A man's life, too, in the course of its development, often brings him into inappropriate situations, in which he finds it difficult to hold his own without danger. Then it is important to be sensible and yielding. This enables him to discover a safe place in which life can go on, although he may be surrounded by danger."[8]

It so happens that the snow goose, like the tundra swan, has been totemic for me, ever since I startled a flock preparing for migration one evening in 1963 as I was walking along the shore of the Bering Sea. A dozen snow white swans lifted off in unison and flew low over the gray waves into the late summer twilight. It was a mystical vision, one that still lives in my heart. This wise counsel of the *I Ching* connected me at a crucial moment to an especially meaningful image and connected me in a way that inspired my perseverance and generated a space of inner tranquility, while suggesting a way to develop in the role of president, step by step. For the next few years, I reminded myself that I was in a position that did not suit me, and I needed always to be on the lookout for sustainable options, the way a bush pilot in Alaska constantly scans the terrain below for likely landing spots, should his single engine fail.

Even before I met Dr. Li in my dream, I had been using him regularly as a consultant in my practice. He is especially useful when confusing transference and countertransference problems arise. I write a full and honest account of the present circumstance and the difficulties as I experience them, not sparing myself details which I might be inclined to gloss over if consulting a fellow professional. By the time I finish writing, I have a clearer notion of my analysand, what I am experiencing, and what aspects of my own unconscious psyche are aroused. I also have a clearer picture of what my analysand may be experiencing! Then I throw the coins. Sometimes, the resulting hexagram is more or less what I anticipated, with the hexagram mirroring the situation or echoing the interpersonal complexity I had just elucidated. Sometimes the result is a complete reversal of my expectations, challenging me to re-evaluate everything. Regardless of the outcome, the *I Ching* stimulates a new line of thinking.

Having been a child without a father, it is often difficult for me to stand up to a difficult situation, to address it reasonably with energy and confidence. Ideally, his role would have been to prepare me for outer life in a reasonable way. Always, I am challenged to do this for myself, especially in the analytic setting, where I have learned

---

8 *The* I Ching *or Book of Changes*, 207.

I can be vulnerable to emotional cues, which might overpower my conscious intent and lead to paralyzing confusion. I can count on the *I Ching* to help me put the task at the center, not my emotional reactions.

One great failing of the good Dr. Li is his patriarchal language, which women know is misogynistic and spoiling in itself. I generally overlook this as a cultural trait of the text, one that requires translation into psychological language. If I can repair the psychological damage done by my abandoning father or mother, I will have the opportunity to heal that old wound and build a more stable internalized father image with my own actions and habits of thought. This will compensate my absent father and free psychic energy from the personal complex, making it available for creative work. The *I Ching* gives me a way to connect with the archetypal unconscious, the source of symbol and mythological imagery. Reflecting on the many images in a single consultation is a kind of Jungian amplification, which alters my perception of the immediate situation. Since how we perceive the world is basic to character formation, this routine practice was re-forming my character.

I find particularly helpful the recently published Eranos Foundation edition of the *I Ching*, entitled *The Original I Ching Oracle*, translated by Ritsema and Sabbadini, because it takes into account the situational relativity of Chinese characters, allowing us to choose the images that resonate with the personal situation under investigation. One is free to do that with the Bollingen *I Ching*, of course, but its metaphors tend to channel thinking and feeling into more definite forms of meaning, toward the embodied archetypal image rather than the archetype-as-such that exists only *in potentia*. For example, the Bollingen *I Ching* uses the term "superior man" for its ideal consultant, whereas the Eranos text uses a Chinese term, "Jun zi," meaning simply "ideal of a person who orders his/her life in accordance with dao, rather than willful intention, and uses divination in this spirit."[9] Over the years, this is how I have approached the *I Ching*, not willing any one answer, but opening myself to its guidance toward the right way, the right attitude in the moment—approaching it without memory or desire, if you will. Over time, the process of reliance on "this great and singular book" has helped me to realize dao in action, which the Eranos translation of the *I Ching* interprets as "acquiring that which makes a being become what it is meant to be."[10] I think this has been my life's work.

---

9 *The Original* I Ching *Oracle*, 762.
10 *The Original* I Ching *Oracle*, 240.

I guess I am trying to tell you what kind of Jungian analyst I am. There are many ways to become the analysts we are becoming. Seminars, consultation, and certification processes got me started. I am grateful to my analysts and to the analysts who certified me in my raw, unfinished state thirty years ago. This work in progress only began then in earnest and continues. Reflecting on a life of literary scholarship, the Canadian critic Northrop Frye shared his belief that a person becomes "what one is through influences"[11] and he suggests choosing a major writer as a kind of spiritual preceptor for the self. He continues, "I am not speaking, of course, of any sort of moral model," he continues, "but it seems to me that growing up inside a mind so large that one has no sense of claustrophobia within it is an irreplaceable experience in humane studies."[12] Indeed, it was a matter of serendipity that in choosing a mate I also stumbled into the spacious minds of Dr. Jung and Dr. Li, but it was perseverance alone that steadied my feet along a path of individuation by their lights. In the *I Ching*'s Hexagram 18, Ku/Work on What Has Been Spoiled [Decay][13] states, "What has been spoiled through man's fault can be made good again through man's work." I can honestly say that I have rarely turned down new opportunities to step into the stream of life and have never drawn back from hard work.

However, I could never have proceeded along that path had I not found able helpers. I have debts of gratitude to many who furthered my individuation story. In Alaska with its wild, vast, and awesome beauty and with the support of generous and intelligent people, I discovered that I had a mind which I enjoyed using! Stanford played its part in stabilizing my identity through offering a chance to test myself against the personal and intellectual challenge of a strong medical education. My fellow Jungian analysts and our Jungian ancestors, in community and in *communitas,* have made the container in which I am becoming the being I was meant to be. Included among that community are the ancient Chinese scholars who worked out a system of divination and refined it over centuries of reflection and revision. Together in the moment of throwing the coins, we are embedded in the same *communitas,* across time and space. Through the archetypal unconscious, wisdom and spiritual states have arisen and danced from soul to soul. Dr. Li is indeed an animate being who gives intelligent answers.

---

11 Northrop, "The Search for Acceptable Words," in *Spiritus Mundi: Essays on Literature, Myth, and Society,* 11.

12 Northrop, "The Search for Acceptable Words," 11–12.

13 *The* I Ching *or Book of Changes,* 75.

Through my long and respectful relationship with this magnificent old text and my responses to its language I have developed a symbolic attitude. It has helped me realize the power of Jung's central vision—that psychological development hinges upon the dynamism of the opposites—and it has helped me hold conflicting impulses and views. It helped me to bear up under fierce emotional states and take the long view, especially along that most difficult spiritual journey—marriage. Each of my several personal analyses has in its own way reshaped the father hole, yet failed to show me a way out. Through the *I Ching,* I have found my own myth, which I believe is to seek the Middle Way. After decades of attention to its wisdom, I have realized that a Philemon-like presence exists just for me, the good Dr. Li.

I would like to end with the final lines of a poem by the former American Poet Laureate, Stanley Kunitz. He wrote "The Layers" when he was in his mid-nineties, and it ends:

> Though I lack the art
>
> to decipher it
>
> no doubt the next chapter
>
> in my book of transformations
>
> is already written
>
> I am not done with my changes.[14]

---

14 For the full text of the poem, "The Layers," by Stanley Kunitz, see the website of the American Academy of Poets at http://www.poets.org/viewmedia.php/prmMID/19250 accessed September 2, 2011.

References

Frye, Northrop. *Spritus Mundi: Essays on Literature, Myth, and Society*. Bloomington: Indiana University Press, 1976/1983.

Jung, C. G.. "Foreword." in *The* I Ching *or Book of Changes*, translated from the Chinese by Richard Wilhelm, English translation by Cary F. Baynes, xxi–xxxix. Princeton: Princeton University Press, 1950/1967.

Ritsema, R., and Sabbadini, S.A., Translators. *The Original* I Ching *Oracle*. New York: Sterling Publishing Co., Inc., 2007.

Old Roots, New Soil

by Chie Lee

The path that led me to Jungian psychology was deeply influenced by the turmoil that surrounded China during my formative years. I was born in Shanghai two years after Mao's revolution had overthrown the Nationalist government. At the time of my birth in 1951, our family was in a precarious state both financially and politically.

My paternal grandfather was a high ranking military man in the Nationalist government. My father was the son of his second wife, who was a half Russian woman from Mongolia. She died at age twenty-four, a month after giving birth to my father. In 1949, my grandfather left with his family for Taiwan as Mao's victory became inevitable. At the time, my father was working as a commercial pilot and stationed in Hong Kong. In 1950 he made a fateful decision that he would regret till the day he died. My father, along with two other pilots, flew a nationalist airline plane back to the mainland, as his answer to the call from the newly established Communist regime to return to China and help build and modernize the Motherland.

After my father's return to Shanghai with my mother, his patriotic zest and optimism were soon crushed and brutal reality set in. My paternal grandfather's military position with the Nationalists in Taiwan, and the fact that my father was the descendant of landowners and had spent time in America, all marked him as capitalist and therefore politically untrustworthy. There were repeated "discussions" with him and many "evaluative sessions." Many would commit suicide after these repeated marathon "evaluative sessions." In October of 1951, about a year after my father's return and seven months after I was born, he was sent away to "re-education" camp. He would never fly an airplane or see me again.

My father and I lost contact for twenty-some years but would reconnect in the late 1970s through correspondence after a cousin of his located me in Los Angeles. Some painful awareness came after we reconnected. I learned that my father had known where we lived in Shanghai but did not contact us all those years for fear of further political scrutiny. In a way, I had always known that he had abandoned me, even while I made up stories to justify his absence from my life. These stories crumbled when I

My parents with me at 7 months old, 1951, Shanghai.

had to accept the fact that he could have contacted me through an uncle and his family who still live in our Shanghai house to this day. My father wrote that after the Cultural Revolution, he felt too ashamed to look up my uncle.

Looking back, I am thankful that we reconnected at a time when my own life was coming unglued, and therefore, although I felt deeply disappointed and pained by his choice to abandon me, I could forgive him and had empathy for his flawed human-ity. The suffering and torture he had to endure during the Cultural Revolution was unspeakable, and he became a cripple after a failed attempt to kill himself.

A sweet memory from that time was a request from my father to send him a pair of Ray-Ban sunglasses and a Ronson cigarette lighter, items that he associated with his training with the U.S. Air Force in California and his years as a pilot, the high points of his life. I did so, and later he sent me a picture of himself wearing the sunglasses, standing proudly in front of the Forbidden City in Beijing. Often when I remember my father, this image of him comes up, and I am comforted.

Before I had a chance to return to China to visit him, my father died of a stroke or massive heart attack at the age of 58. He died alone in the dorm of the factory where he lived, a broken man who had survived the brutality of the Cultural Revolution.

The issue of the "father" and the relationship to the inner as well as the outer masculine has been a core struggle in my psychological development, suffused with ambivalence, confusion, disappointments, and unmet longings. A recent memory around "father" comes to mind: I was with my cousin and his family hiking in the Sierras. We came across a splendid vista of snow-capped mountains and deep blue lakes. The beauty was exhilarating. My cousin was with his college-age daughter, and I could see in the way he looked at her how excited he was that they were sharing this special moment. In a surprised state of confused emotions, my eyes started to well up. Later, when I was alone and sat with my feelings, I knew I felt envious. But, at the deepest level, I was very sad and will always grieve what I will never know: being held in a loving gaze by the father. The insufficient personal experiences had encased the father in a primordial force field and did and can still wreak havoc in my life.

Until I was eighteen, I grew up among three generations of women: my maternal grandmother, my aunt and her daughter, my older sister, and a maid that had been with the family before I was born. After my father was sent away, my mother became the breadwinner in the family. We left Shanghai in 1958 and lived separately from her. My mother had a series of businesses in Southeast Asia and lived in Bangkok while the rest of us settled in Macao. She would visit for a month or so each year, descending on us kids with presents and treats. She was like a movie star: beautiful, cosmopolitan, and glamorous. Although I did not physically spend much time with my mother during those years, she was a formidable presence in all our lives, both feared and loved.

My grandmother and aunt were intimidated by my mother during those visits. My mother expected devotion and attention from all, but dissatisfaction would inevitably surface after a few weeks. Her temper would flare up, and she would then remind all of us that we were alive only because she worked hard and suffered so that she could send us a check every month. Yes, the memory of that expected check! The family would begin to anticipate its arrival by the fifteenth of each month. The tension at home would rise palpably as each day passed. Then one day I would come home from school and know that the check had come, because the apartment would smell wonderful from a fresh chicken stewing in the pot, and my grandmother had a smile on her face. We would all live for another month!

My mother was the oldest girl, with three younger siblings. From a young age, her fierce personality and temper terrified her family. The only person that could "tame" her was my maternal grandfather, and they adored each other. This grandfather was a merchant and traveled frequently for long periods of time. He died from typhoid fever when my mother was fourteen. The family soon began to face financial hardship, and my mother, being the oldest, left high school and began working at sixteen to support the family. She married my sister's father quite young as his third wife. He was a very wealthy businessman, and although the relationship did not last, my mother was comfortably provided for as the mother of his daughter.

My parents met in 1947 and fell in love. My mother was part of Shanghai's social scene, known for her beauty and style, and my father was a handsome young pilot who had just returned from America. Their marriage, from stories told to me by my aunt, was passionate yet tortuous. It was not sustainable, and I believe they would not have stayed together even if my father had not been sent away.

My mother is now ninety and currently lives near Los Angeles in an assisted living facility, afflicted with advanced dementia. My mother has had difficulty in almost all of the significant relationships in her life; ours was especially troubled. It has only been in these last years, as her dementia reached such a severe state and her fierceness has almost disappeared, that I can finally relax in her presence.

I am also increasingly aware, with horror, that I share some of her personality traits; many of them are ones I couldn't stand in her. My mother and I both have a combustible and fiery energy. Her style is "slash and burn," and I have never known her to apologize or acknowledge her shortcomings. I have had the good fortune of many years of analysis to help contain the "fire" and grasp those negative aspects of my personality. I can still "combust" but can hold myself to suffer the consequence and thus maybe incur less damage to my relationships than she did.

As I have had to suffer and tolerate my own shortcomings, my compassion for my mother has deepened. She was indeed a very flawed person and we, the other women in the family, in varying degrees all suffered from her abuse of the power she had over us. But my mother was also right: we survived those treacherous years because she possessed such fierce survival and life instinct. It was remarkable that with limited education and no employable skill, she still managed to make a living and kept us alive.

I believe that my sister and I both inherited that determination and will to live, which was an invaluable inner resource and which supported us through many losses and tribulations when we embarked on our journey in a strange new country. Perhaps my venturing into Jungian psychology was a continuation of this "wandering and exploring"; this time it was exploring the new landscape of the unconscious. Through having to negotiate and survive forces beyond my personal control, the Jungian paradigm that the Self and not the ego is at the center of the individual spoke powerfully to me.

With my grandmother in Macau: from left to right: my cousin, my sister, and me.

I grew up with a sense that my family was different. We had no father or mother at home, and we all had different surnames. I either avoided the subject of my parents or made up stories that made our family seem "normal." Most of my friends never met my mother, because I didn't want them to ask me questions about her.

When I was around eleven and my sister and cousin were both sixteen, we decided that instead of having three different surnames, we would officially change our names. I remember that the three of us informed my grandmother and aunt about our decision, filled out the necessary forms, and chose our own names. We chose our maternal family name as our surname. Then we each chose one character from the dictionary that appealed to us, with the criterion that all the characters had a similar visual structure, but different meaning. I chose "Chie," which meant a type of rock. Looking back, we were creating a familial linkage that could show the world we were not a disparate but a cohesive unit. In a way, the three of us reinvented ourselves, started afresh with new identities, and took a step toward the creation of our own destiny.

When I was sixteen, after living in Bangkok for two years, I moved to Hong Kong and was alone with my grandmother. My sister, with the help of a Jesuit priest in Macao, left to attend college in Glendale, California. My cousin married and moved to Taiwan. My mother and aunt continued to live in Bangkok, struggling to make a living after my mother's hotel laundry business failed. In Hong Kong my grandmother and I rented one room from a family and lived there for two years until I finished high school. It was the loneliest time of my life, and to this day it pains me to remember those days. My grandmother was bearing most of the stress of managing our hand-to-mouth existence. Now in her mid-seventies, she still couldn't escape her life of having to "eat bitterness."

My maternal grandmother had been betrothed to my grandfather when she was one year old. She was from a family of respectability and means and the only child. Her father died when she was very young. She had a relatively pampered childhood, with tutors who taught her calligraphy and classic literature. I grew up admiring the elegance of her calligraphy; mine is awful, for I never heeded her prompting to practice my brush stokes. My grandmother endured a few years of suffering the tortuous process of having her feet bound until my great-grandmother, in defiance of the male elders, un-bound her daughter's feet. The crippling effect of those few years of forced deformation of her feet left her with lifelong pain in her feet, joints, and back. Cold and gray days would find me massaging her feet and her knees for a fee, and I would always recoil at their grotesque shape no matter how many times I'd touched them.

My grandmother was afflicted with Alzheimer's disease in her last years. My sister and I paid for her to return to Shanghai, to be cared for by my uncle and his family. I returned to Shanghai in 1980 to see her. She did not know who I was, and she died two years later. I cry when memories of my grandmother well up. Those are tears for the unrelenting bitter life she had to bear, for the loss of the only person who loved me without condition, and for the generations of Chinese women, like her, whose suffering and endurance are my legacy.

When I graduated at eighteen and did quite well in my exams to qualify for university, I was in utter despair, because there were no financial means for me to further my education. The only path that I could envision was to become a secretary and then marry a decent man. My whole future seemed to be mapped out already, and it felt like a dead end. I wrote to my sister, and she stepped forth and changed my life. She told me that if I could get together a one-way ticket and a visa, I could live with her, and she and I would figure out the next step together. I seized the opportunity. So in 1969, with twenty dollars in my pocket and terrified, I arrived in Los Angeles.

The first stop was Burbank, California. My sister was attending California State University at night and worked during the day. She and I lived with the family of an orthopedic surgeon who at the time was separated from his wife. In return for free room and board, my sister and I cooked breakfast and dinner. I attended Burbank High School as a senior, mainly to improve my English. My cooking was terrible! The son would look at what I cooked, politely say he was not hungry, and disappeared. Grandpa did not complain, mainly because with me there he did not have to eat alone. While I ate my food quietly, he would tell me how much he missed his wife, who had died a few years before. At the opposite side of the house, sitting alone at the bar staring out at a panoramic and glittering view of Burbank, the surgeon sat and drank.

This first year in Burbank was an initiation into an "otherness" which was American culture and values. I was painfully isolated and was in a chronic state of anxiety from the moment I woke up. Every day, I thought about returning to my grandmother. But instinctively, I knew I could never return, for the desire to attend university and have a better life was more compelling, and I persevered. Home was already lost to me when our family left Shanghai and joined the Chinese diaspora. For a long time, and in some way still continuing to this day, I belonged to neither the Chinese nor the American culture, yet I was and still am deeply affected by both.

One year later my sister and I moved in with another more "functional" American family. I worked at two jobs to finance my education at University of Southern California and graduated with a degree in dental hygiene. Seemingly I had become another immigrant success story. But the adaptation process and the unrelenting anxieties had exacted their toll. Physical and psychic fragmentation was just around the corner.

When I was twenty-five, I met a Chinese dentist who shared my family background and struggles. Six months after we met we were married. The marriage began to unravel almost immediately, and we were divorced after three years. Years later I had some insight into the state of my mind, into why I would choose to marry a man after knowing him only a few months. A memory came to mind: I was twenty-four and arrived from California at the Honolulu airport. I was alone and looking forward to my first vacation since I had left Hong Kong six years before. I looked around and saw all the Asian faces, and all of a sudden, for the first time in years, my whole body relaxed. They all looked like me! The following year, I met this young dentist whom I felt was my kin. Like me, he was born in Shanghai, and his family became financially destitute after 1949. He also came to America alone and worked jobs to put himself through UCLA dental school. I relaxed and felt at home with him. I did not have to be vigilant and scan faces to make sure I was doing what was expected. With him I was not "Other."

The disconnect from the cultural and ancestral layers of my psyche, the longing for home, for a sense of community and belonging, were some other forces that brought me to Jungian psychology. The adaptation process and the constant state of self scrutiny during my first twelve years in the U.S. left me in a state of fragmentation and a precarious psychological condition. I was at the mercy of whatever forces that would constellate in my life. Finally, at thirty, after surviving a rejected boyfriend's murderous rage, holding me at knife point for hours, I was utterly exhausted and defeated. After a week in the hospital with a serious blood infection, I had a moment of clarity: I had no control over my life. I was lost and in a state of impoverishment of both body and soul.

During this floundering time, a friend came in to have her teeth cleaned and left me a brochure of public programs offered by the Los Angeles Jung Institute. A seminar on dreams caught my attention. I signed up for the class and went to it every week at the home of a Jungian analyst. For those two months I sat and listened and comprehended very little. Yet I was mesmerized. I had no knowledge of Jungian psychology and had never recorded my dreams until then. The whole seminar was like a dream.

Thus began my passionate reading of Jung and other Jungian writers. I attended numerous seminars at both the Los Angeles and the San Francisco Jung Institute. Six years after my first dream seminar, with a clarity that astounded me, I decided that I wanted to become a Jungian analyst. I had married the year before, and my life had entered a phase of stability that supported this arduous venture. I enrolled in graduate school and began my twelve-year journey from graduate school to certification as Jungian analyst.

Steve and I at Jung's Bollingen Tower, Switzerland, 1997.

My husband is a third-generation Chinese-American who grew up in Oakland, California. He is a professor of pathology at UCLA. How we became a couple was truly synchronistic. A mutual friend introduced us, he being newly separated and I, divorced. Nothing happened until a few months later, when we found that we were both at a UCLA extension class on Buddhism. He had signed up only because a few days before he had missed a long anticipated trip to Sikkim by mixing up the departure date. We began dating. That was twenty-nine years ago.

My husband read Freud and Jung when he was in high school, but chose to go into medicine and pathology as a career. Our relationship rekindled his old interest in psychology, and he embarked on a parallel journey in Jungian studies. He read, attended seminars, had a long analysis, and faithfully kept a dream journal filled with images.

There were challenges and struggles in our years together. I believe our marriage endured and is solid because our psychological work enabled us each to retrieve some projections and hold more objective perspectives of each other's shortcomings. I feel blessed that I finally have a relationship with a man who accepts me as I am and who can stand solidly in place and not turn away when I am at my worst.

My first analysis was with a male analyst. My conscious life then was guided mostly by my thinking and sensation function, and my self-worth was rooted in what and how much I did. My analyst was about my father's age, a feeling-intuitive type, with a lot of fire in his personality. We worked together for almost eight years and ended in a rupture that was devastating to me. It was a re-experiencing of my abandonment by the father. As I began to integrate the experience a few years later through a second analysis, I accepted that psychically the re-wounding was fated to occur. For as the analytic processes deepened, we descended down into the primal layer of narcissistic longings and defenses and my distrust of the father/masculine crashed in. The subsequent humanizing of my relationship with my first analyst served to personalize the primordial father energy, and some healing of the split in my psyche between the idealized and the disappointing "father" was experienced and integrated. For that I am deeply grateful.

A dream came in 2011 while I was writing this essay:

My husband and I were walking by my first analyst's office building, which was a bungalow. I told my husband to look at the tree in front of the large window, which I had previously told him about. This tree was lush and beautifully trained into a wide fan shape that covered the window. It provided enough privacy, but the feathered foliage also allowed for ample light to stream through. Then I saw my first analyst at the window, and he waved at me to come in. I went in and saw my second and still current analyst sitting with her back to me in the sofa. I excused myself and left.

I woke up with a gentle feeling of joy. The dream had a golden haze around the tree and the bungalow was light and open. (My memory of my first analyst's bungalow office was quite different.) The psychic landscape of my analytic experiences has changed. There is now more consciousness, receptivity, and a convergence of my inner split. My "analysts," man and woman, are talking to each other!

By the summer of 2011, I had served the first year of a two-year term as the president of the Jung Institute of Los Angeles. I often think about why I have been so devoted to my Jungian community in these last ten years after my certification as a Jungian analyst. The many personal connections with people of the community matter and are of great value to me. But at the core of this devotion is a profound feeling of gratitude that this is where I can belong, for the multicultural, expansive, and deep container that is Jungian psychology can hold the core Self of this confused and hybrid amalgamation that is me. I have found my village.

Section Four
Dark Night of the Body

He who contemplates the darkness in himself, to him the light is near.
—The Red Book

A Truchas Story: I toss and turn these nights—the room too hot, the day before too stimulating. Finally I ask my guides to help me sleep, and at 4 a.m. I fall into a slumber and dream I have started a fire in my writing studio. I ask my son to call the fire department, but by the time they arrive, the building is engulfed in flames. I fear for the fate of my goats, who share the building with my studio. Later I learn that although they have been injured, a vet is taking care of them.

Disturbed, when I awaken I journal, talk to Donald, to Naomi. My goats are those animals that connect me to physicality and its joys. The fires of creativity could take everything. P.D.

Karlyn Ward: *Voices*

Henry Abramovitch: *Into the Marginal Zone*

Sharon Heath: *The Church of Her Body*

Karlyn Ward, Henry Abramovitch, and Sharon Heath tell haunting stories of the difficult business of getting body and soul aligned. In Ward's case, it is her mother's body and soul that have been at odds all her life, casting a terrible shadow. Although Abramovitch is in Israel and Heath in Los Angeles, there is a resonance in their struggles to find meaning in their illnesses. For both, their bodily wounding becomes a path to their creativity.

VOICES

by Karlyn M. Ward

One of the great gifts of Jungian thought is that it allows for the possibility of holding the most difficult, dark, charged, and even shocking of life's experiences in larger contexts—symbolically, metaphorically, and archetypally—toward understanding, forgiveness, and perhaps even transformation.

On an ordinary Tuesday morning my first patient began her hour by asking, "Have you ever had to give your own mother an enema?"

I couldn't have felt more empathic, and was aware of how my own life experiences contribute to my understanding of my patients—even this.

Ten years earlier, my mother, who lived on the Olympic Peninsula in Washington state, announced that she had decided to have knee replacement surgery in San Francisco so she could convalesce in our modest suburban town house with its two full flights of stairs. The unspoken assumption: all her friends recovered from illnesses at the homes of their children, so she would too. In fact, her own mother-in-law, after a hip replacement, had gone to live permanently with her daughter whose home, incidentally, was perhaps four times the size of ours, and accessible for the disabled.

So we made adjustments and arrangements, and, following surgery, my mother began her convalescence in our small living room-turned-bedroom.

Most days I saw patients until 8:30 p.m., and only then came home, tired and hungry, ready for dinner and downtime.

However, on this Thursday, the first thing I heard, while climbing the stairs from the front entrance, was my mother's familiar martyred voice and her unexpected greeting, "I guess you'll just have to give me an enema."

Not even a cursory "Hi, how was your day?"

"I need a cup of tea," I said, while thinking the only expletive appropriate to the situation.

84

While it's true she was physically constipated and in distress, eventually I came to see the enema incident as a metaphor. Like physical constipation, emotional constipation implies something blocked, inability to release something dark.

Like the enema, it would be up to me, over time, to resolve it through a personal alchemical *solutio*, dissolving perhaps generations of impacted material so the flow and passage could proceed more freely, and the process would take an unexpected turn.

Eleven years later I went to Washington to be with my mother, who was dying. She had already dismantled the home in which she and my father had lived for twenty-five years, with its accumulation of contents of fifty-six years of marriage and thirteen of widowhood, and had moved into a senior residence, where she had lived for just six months.

The next move was to the hospital, and only four days later, transfer to a convalescent hospital for "terminal care." This may sound preposterous to some, but it has been standard medical practice (read "travesty") for years. Since I had worked a decade as a medical social worker, I was not surprised at this turn of events, but I was once again furious with the depersonalization of the medical system and with the fact that this transfer took place without my permission.

Now she was dying in fits and starts. One day, all of us, including the medical staff, would be sure this was "it." The following day she would be carrying on as usual.

My home life and analytic practice were disrupted as I made unscheduled trips to her bedside. I'd always been ambivalent about being an only child, and this was no exception. While I was free to make decisions without the interference and outer conflict that can arise among siblings at such times, there also were no siblings to be allies, to share the responsibility, the decision-making, the grief, or the family stories. My husband and adult children were wonderful consultants, but respectfully left the decisions to me.

During this time, the Olympic Peninsula was in full splendor, the waters of Puget Sound sparkling, the sun shining on the snow-peaked Olympic Mountains, which I'd always found a source of strength and inspiration. The poem I had written after my father's death thirteen years earlier expressed my feelings now, as I attended my remaining parent:

The mountains
the everlasting mountains
reminding me
each time I left the hospital
of the eternal.
Thank you for dying
where there are mountains.

Music came to my mind as well: "I will lift up mine eyes to the hills from whence cometh my help." My mother, an accomplished lyric soprano soloist, had often sung an arrangement of this beautiful verse from Psalm 121.

On one of her better days during this time, my mother wistfully asked, "Do you think I could sing for my own memorial?" We had recordings of some of her performances. It was the best of her, so why not? It was the voice she wanted remembered.

In the intervals when I was at home, music, as always, played a major role for me. This time it was the massive Mahler *8th Symphony* that played repeatedly on my car tape recorder. Music is almost always present in my inner world. Like Nature, it has the capacity to connect me to the Self, the central organizing principle of the psyche, and to carry the god-image. But especially when a piece arises spontaneously in my mind, like the Mahler, I try to understand its meaning for this particular moment in my life. I'd long loved the Mahler 8th, and knew it well, having performed it as a member of the chorus. Subtitled "The Symphony of a Thousand," this work is scored for full orchestra, eight soloists, double chorus, and children's chorus. It is one of the most massive works in the classical repertoire. The strong, powerful vertical structure of Part I summons the creative spirit … *Veni Creator Spiritus*. Surely I needed its strength to help my dying mother and to sustain me through this rite of passage. Part II, Mahler's treatment of the final scene from Goëthe's *Faust*, flows more horizontally, culminating in the eternal divine feminine leading us onward … *Das ewig Weibliche hinan* … The eternal Feminine, so obscured in my mother, was something I'd had to find for myself over many years.

While learning the piece, I'd tried to share my excitement with my mother and spoke to her of its stunning complexities. She called me a snob. Once again I had realized how impossible it had been to share my deepest feelings with her.

My mother was often critical. When she first heard a recording of my adult, partially trained, singing voice, she exclaimed, "Why, *that's* not your voice!" as though I had intruded into her territory and was impinging upon her ground as "the soloist," apparently arousing her envy and competition. The sad thing was that I always had wanted her approval, but my life had developed in ways she was unprepared to understand or accept.

Now my mother was 86 and I was 61, and the pattern showed little sign of releasing its grip. One day I walked into her hospital room with a notebook I'd had to buy to keep track of the myriad details I had to attend to—end-of-life decisions like moving her possessions, funeral arrangements, financial matters, questions for the doctor, and the list of family and friends to be informed.

Her first comment was typically disdainful, "Always the professional with her notebook!" I shrugged it off, saying mildly there was a lot to tend to. It was all the more painful since I bought this book in service of her care.

But also there were unexpectedly good moments, rare in our relationship. She told me she'd been walking down the hall of her residence and felt a "gentle touch" on her shoulder, then another. When she turned, no one was there. She thought, "It was the Lord, calling me, and telling me it's 'time.'" And so I was able to share with her the dream I'd had six months earlier as I'd been helping her move:

> Seated in her living room was a man who I understood was an angel, telling me, "Now is the time."[1]

Another day she told me she loved me, the first time, ever, I could recall that happening spontaneously. She also told my children what a "prince" my new husband was—her highest form of praise.

The next morning her roommate reported that my mother had been singing in her sleep, ending with an "Alleluia." Later that day she cried and thanked me for doing so much for her. She said she sometimes went into a deep, dark place where she was not

---

1 I'd had other dreams that turned out to be precognitive. In fact, during that same period of time I'd also dreamed of running down the street, having missed my appointment with Marie-Louise von Franz. I awoke, wondering if von Franz had died; it was later confirmed that she had. One can't know at the time whether such dreams are really advance warnings. Until events unfold, you must hold all possibilities, viewing the dream as a message about your own inner world *and* also as the potential for things to come.

sure she still was alive. I wanted to put my head on her shoulder and cry, but I didn't feel close enough to her to do so.

She had been in the convalescent hospital about two weeks, just time enough to become accustomed to the new facility and the staff caring for her, when suddenly I learned that she and the entire Medicare unit were to be moved across the hall. It didn't seem a problem until an empathic nurses' aide whispered to me it would mean dealing with a whole new medical staff. It happened to be a day that my mother had been unresponsive, and we thought she might go at any moment.

My mother's extraverted, effervescent friend and musical colleague Sally, a frequent visitor, was outraged. Sally was a superb church organist, far overqualified for their small town church and its electronic organ. I, too, had been an organist, and respected her huge talent. That day I needed her outrage. I was so worn down I simply started to cry.

Just then I realized some other woman was speaking to me.

Through my tears I glimpsed a name tag that identified her as the Director of Nurses. She had the power to help us, so I took the opportunity: the room my mother was being moved to was not quieter, as had been promised, and surely it wasn't right to make such changes in her environment when she seemed so close to death. The Director of Nurses said she'd "see what she could do."

Thanks to her intervention (and that of the aide—blessed be the aides), my mother was moved into a large, lovely private room, to be cared for by the staff she knew. The crisis resolved, the Director of Nurses, Sally, and I began arranging my mother's possessions in various parts of the room. My mother had remained unresponsive during the move.

Suddenly, from the bed where my mother's body lay unconscious, came a cold, commanding, authoritative, hollow, loud masculine voice:

THERE IS NO DEATH

This was my mother's voice, yet *not* her voice. *Her* voice had been co-opted by an "*other*," in this bold and clearly articulated pronouncement.[2]

---

2 No conventional font, or size of font, could do justice to the magnitude of this utterance. This font seems at least to convey the hollowness of tone. Even when I've tried to imitate

All three of us ran to the bedside, the Director of Nurses gasping, "Oh my goodness, oh my goodness!" I grabbed my notebook—*the* notebook— to record her exact words—with the split-second reasoning that they might be appropriate for a memorial service. My mother remained utterly motionless. Then, the same voice proclaimed:

NO ONE CAN EVER DIE

I repeated hopefully, "No, no one can die." But then, the voice continued:

YOU ALL LIVE ON FOREVER . . .

IN HELL

So much for using her words at a memorial service! The Director of Nurses, visibly shaken, left. Sally, for once, was speechless.

I felt immediate amazement, relief, and understanding, but could share them with no one in the room. I was deeply grateful for many years of Jungian analysis, with my particular analyst. Without them I would not have had a framework for understanding this experience, and it might not have happened. I knew then as I know now: I heard the *voice* of the diabolical archetype that my mother must have defended against her whole life.[3] Awful and powerful as the words were, they also were a gift, a confirmation of the level of unrelatedness I experienced throughout my lifetime—and of the living hell that my mother was experiencing in her final illness.

I was glad to have witnesses, even though they didn't have the same understanding of these "unusual" events. I could never have made this up.

When my daughter arrived a short time later, Sally made light of these "utterances" and the three of us carried on as usual. We even laughed about how my mother's "performance" had added to my own (my earlier tears and confrontation with the nursing director). Perhaps they assumed my mother was suffering from senile dementia, but I knew she was not.

---

the voice out loud, I cannot do it justice. But I never will forget it.

3 Technically, one never sees or hears the actual archetype, since it is an underlying *pattern* of image and affect, but one sees or hears its culturally determined *image*, or in this case, its *voice,* the voice of the diabolical.

Whatever the others thought, for me everything had changed.

When I was alone with my mother a short time later, and deep in thought, my instinct took over. I turned in her direction and said firmly to "it,"

"Release her. *Release her.* **You release her from hell!**"

I stood at her bedside, made the sign of the cross over her, and insisted,

"GET OUT OF HER . . . NOW!"

A few hours later she was awake and miserable, with no memory at all of this experience.

The next morning, my mother asked me to tell her the day and year, and then exclaimed, "And I'm still here? This is awful. I can't believe this. Is there nothing they can do (to help me out of it)?" I wrote in my journal:

> I never thought I'd be in this position (my mother asking me for a way out). A pillow over the face? A nice shot of morphine? I wish—but there's no way.

What was the meaning of all this? I hoped, on a psychic level, something significant was happening for her. Certainly it was for me. Though I doubt the Voice meant to be helpful, it did give me the opportunity to approach my mother problem at a deeper level. A wise friend later suggested that my mother was enduring hell now so she wouldn't have to later, in her own version of the afterlife. Many years afterward, a colleague suggested, "You healed her." I'd like to think a benevolent spirit was acting through me. Or perhaps the evil spirit was exiting her psyche as she was about to die, and it simply wanted the last word.

The next day, my daughter and I were so exhausted we joked about racing to the nearest empty bed, in that "dark" humor that often accompanies crisis. But now we found my mother had grown agitated, and was in considerable pain and discomfort. Though my mother tended to play to an audience, this was no longer the case. She simply didn't have the strength.

Now, just when he was most needed, my mother's doctor had gone on a scheduled vacation, but left no one to cover for him. Further, we were told the medical director of the convalescent hospital was not responsible for covering for absent doctors, and besides, he "couldn't be reached."

Though my mother was getting worse by the moment, members of the nursing staff said their hands were tied.

Though a physician I respected was on duty, she could not take over my mother's care. Whatever medical protocol left us in this limbo made no sense to me.

The staff, trying to be helpful, then suggested we try the local emergency room. Take a dying woman to an emergency room on a Friday night because no one will take responsibility for managing her pain???!!! Now I was livid.

Meanwhile, my mother asked that we take her home with us to California—impossible at this stage.

At this point, Sally was having her own crisis about playing for the funeral. I wanted to scream, and did, in the first private place I could find. (Sometimes it helps.)

Finally, the supervisor arrived. This woman had pleasantly showed us around the facility when my mother was first admitted. Now, her face closed and "professional," she listened as I told our story, calmly and factually, asking innocently if this neglect might be case of medical malpractice. She caught my shot across the bow, and closed down even further. However, within minutes she did reach the medical director, who prescribed sufficient pain medication.

The doctor of my choice was finally able to step in and was stunned at the violation of the doctor-patient relationship. She empathized with us, noting, "This is not a quick and easy demise." Since the situation could last days or weeks, she encouraged me to go home to California and rest, and promised she'd be in touch by phone. She was one of the gifts of the whole experience.

When Sally realized I was leaving, she chided, "You have only one mom . . ."

What came out of my mouth surprised even me: "I've lived with guilt all my life and I'm not going to now."

(When I read this chapter to others, at this moment a votive candle holder cracked and broke, and the fire spilled onto the table in front of us! I was reminded of Jung's experience of feeling red-hot anger while arguing with Freud—the argument that was followed by a loud *CRACK!* in his bookcase.(*Memories, Dreams, Reflections,* p. 155) At that moment, my old persona, the one that would never have given such a response, may finally have shattered like the glass holding the votive candle.)

Sally and her friends spoke so enthusiastically about my "mom," but it never occurred to me to call her that. I thought of a mom as someone you easily could talk to, whose love was palpable. Generally this was not my experience of my mother, and the idea of calling her "mom" had never been discussed. A wise woman mentor pointed out that this ideal mom was their lie, and not my truth.

Yet what my mother couldn't give me, she did give to my daughter, and I was grateful for her experience of her grandmother. My mother once said, "The reason grandparents and grandchildren get along so well is that they have a common enemy." She was only partly joking.

My mother finally was released from life—after enduring a huge abdominal mass, intestinal obstruction, massive bleeding, and the horrendous itching that comes with kidney failure. At the end, she literally itched to get out of her skin.

At first, along with the numbness and exhaustion of grief, I felt a profound sense of relief, and heard echoing in my mind, "Ding dong, the witch is dead." But that was only a portion of the truth. I was grieving not only my mother, but also the mother I never had.

Often it is only after a difficult parent leaves the world that one can find a measure of equanimity. Since her death, I have found increasing compassion for the triumph and tragedy of my mother's life. She moved away from the small town where she was raised and developed a kind of sophistication, living in different parts of the country, successfully making new friends, and singing professionally.

But how hard she must have worked unconsciously to keep this negative force at bay. Whatever "the sins of the fathers" had been, they emerged undisguised in the Voice. She spent her whole life defending against it as best she could. She did such a good job that most people never suspected the darkness she carried within her—and neither did she.

Through the Voice, I understood with crystal clarity what must have been the desperation of my mother's life: the persistent threat of domination by a negative archetype. She sought refuge in its opposites: conventional religious beliefs and in her lovely, heartfelt singing.

Yet it broke through in unexpected ways. In my early childhood, I had intimations of this archetype and its raw power. In one horrific nightmare, I was chased by the Devil. During World War II, my mother "teased" me, insisting that she was a Nazi.

Once, while in the driver's seat, she got into a single-car, never-understood accident that nearly killed us all, after which she wouldn't drive for years.

Sometimes the archetype takes over, and leaves the poor human being to pay the price.

Sometime after the encounter with the Voice, I began a letter to my children:

It's not that I didn't love your grandmother.

I did, but in a complex way.

Into the Marginal Zone

by Henry Abramovitch

PART ONE - BECOMING A JUNGIAN ANALYST

One Day in September

My pathway to becoming a Jungian analyst began one day in September. I walked into the master bedroom and found my mother, her exquisitely beautiful blue eyes staring up at the corner of the ceiling. Strange, I thought. Then I realized she was not breathing. Using my water safety training, I tried to give her the kiss of life, but her entire passageway was clogged. Using an alternative form of artificial respiration, I held her flaccid hands together with mine and pressed down hard on her diaphragm. From out of her mouth came a fountain of vomit. My brother was with me and said, "She's gone."

"No!" I screamed back. But she was. Dead. In one moment, I became a hero crushed down by failure to save my mother and by my inability to make sense of her senseless, sudden death. I was barely 21.

Madagascar

Still bearing the weight of an enormous mother complex, I looked for ways to come to terms with her loss. As an anthropologist-psychologist, I searched for a society that knew how to make peace with the dead. I stumbled across Madagascar, the island continent off the east coast of Africa. How I got there is a story in itself, but once I found my place on a small island, I became immersed in spirit possession healing and rituals surrounding death.

In this culture, burial at the time of death is a relatively simple affair, but years later, the entire extended family and clan gather in the cemetery for the *fahamadiana* or "second burial." The white bones of the deceased are dug up from the earth and laid out on a woven reed mat. The head of the lineage goes down on one knee and speaks to the soul of the dead relative, saying, "See, we have not forgotten you; look how many people are here; look how much ancestral beer we have made ready in your honor." After he makes his peace with the spirit of the deceased, he turns to call on all the great ancestors, the *razabe*, to receive this "fresh soul" in the midst of the family as a junior ancestor. Then everyone—young men and old men, young women and old women—start drinking and dancing ecstatically in the cemetery. Some may even dance with the bones, rewrapped in the white cloth and the reed mat. The bones are placed in a wooden or cement sarcophagus that resembles their huts, so that the cemetery looks like a miniature village for the dead. Infertile women prize the reed mat upon which the bones had lain for its fertility powers, so much so that contact with the dead is seen as a source of living vitality. I had always associated graveyards with separation and sadness. Yet this ritual of becoming an ancestor remains the most joyous event I ever witnessed. I am still struck, many years later, by how the most important event in their life cycle occurs years after they are dead, when they become ancestors.

A Resurrection Experience

The Malagasy are wonderfully friendly and open people but have a dark xenophobic shadow. Naively, I did not realize that I was entering deeply into cultural secrets that certain people did not want me to know. One day, following a terrible bout of diarrhea, I became confused and found myself drinking salt water, wandering aimlessly, unable to concentrate, and thinking that I was going to die. Passing out, I had an unusual vision: I had indeed died and was buried, and the process of bodily disintegration had begun. My dead body was being pulled apart by worms, moles, and insects. Suddenly, a voice called out, "Stop!" The process was halted and then reversed. My decomposed body was reconstituted, revived, and resurrected, rather like in a shamanistic initiation. I had other intense psychotic-like visions and eventually found my way to a clinic and then to a hospital. I was told that I might have been poisoned. Because I was a foreigner, the culprit had given me enough poison to get rid of me but not to kill me. Whatever actually happened, I was deeply traumatized and recovered very slowly. My persona had been stripped away. I could not travel by myself, and my sister had to come and take me home. I had left Madagascar, but my soul had not yet caught up.

When I finally managed to return to my university and told the story of my experiences and visions to one of my professors, he said, "You would be a good candidate for Jungian analysis." One of my doctoral supervisors, Daniel Levinson, had discovered Jung via his own midlife crisis and had done pioneering work on adult development, summarized in *The Seasons of a Man's Life*. He suggested that I see a Jungian colleague who was part of his research team, Ray Walker, who had trained at the C.G. Jung Institute of New York. We started working on my dreams, and I felt I had arrived back "home" at last.

When I finished my doctoral studies, I decided I needed to take a moratorium. What followed was an important year that included a trip to my ancestral roots in Romania and hitchhiking around Eastern Europe with my sister. I remember the moment at which I actually decided to become a Jungian analyst. I was in Rome, staying with my friends in The Living Theatre, an international political theatre group. I found Jung's *Memories, Dreams, Reflections*, opened it at random, and read that ancestors represented the realm of the collective unconscious.[1] It was a Eureka moment for me: "Yes, that's it!"

The Dream

I traveled by slow boat to Israel, where the intensity of human relations and the austere Biblical beauty of Jerusalem grabbed me. I found a new analyst, William Alex, recently arrived from San Francisco and one of the first graduates of the Zurich Institute. I had strong, positive transference to him as a warm, loving father figure who helped me descend into the underworld. Later, I applied to train in the Israel Association of Analytical Psychology, founded by Erich Neumann in the 1950s. Suddenly I had second thoughts. I wondered whether I really wanted to spend so much time, energy, and money in this enterprise. Then I had a dream:

> I am wandering through a medieval European city, through narrow alleyways and along high walls. Then I walk up some steps and come to a heavy wooden door. I go up to the door and knock. The door opens. Jung himself opens the door and invites me in. We are standing in the hallway that is also a little museum, with beautiful artifacts revealed behind sliding glass doors. Jung slides open one of the panels and gives me a beautiful artifact.

1 C.G. Jung, *Memories, Dreams, Reflections*, p. 216.

When I awoke, I knew I had to do the training.

PART TWO - INTO THE MARGINAL ZONE

What's Wrong with Your Eye?

I completed my training and enjoyed my work as an analyst for almost twenty years until something happened for which neither my analysis nor my training had prepared me. I discovered that my left eyelid was drooping. I felt no pain, no discomfort, and only became aware of it when a neighbor noticed a flaw in my persona and said, "What's wrong with your eye?"

I went to numerous doctors—ophthalmologists, neurologists, and internists—and underwent many tests, none of which uncovered the cause. At the same time, I began losing weight, eating less, and lacking my usual bounce. Sleeping became painful due to what I later discovered was a hugely swollen spleen and liver. One day I became breathless. I could not even walk up a single flight of stairs. Still, I felt it would pass; it was nothing to be worried about. I even traveled abroad to give a workshop. When I returned, suddenly my white blood cell count jumped to "panic levels."

The next day, or rather night—thanks to my wife's persistence—I meet with a hematologist. I sit with her in a deserted cancer institute. We talk, and she explains what a lymph node does—I barely knew, but soon my muse understood:

> Neutrophils are the butterflies, coming and going like a summer day,
> Landing on the trees of acute infection.
> Lymphocytes are the reserves and reconnaissance that fight
> Chronic conditions and recall previous invaders.
> Slow and steady they try to win the race
> They are tortoises of the immune system.

Then she said, "Lets look at the blood slides together." She took me to her lab, drew blood, and when the slides were ready, she took a deep breath, took a look, and said, "Oh, they are cute." She had suspected a fatal, highly aggressive blood disease but had found instead a slow-growing, "indolent" lymphoma.

There are at least 45 different subtypes of lymphoma, each with its own treatment and prognosis. Whereas a diagnosis is usually achieved via a lymph biopsy, this procedure was not possible in my case. For a whole month, I had almost daily tests to discover what had been brewing in my body. On the day of the bone marrow biopsy, I called my medical colleague to ask him to fill in for my teaching. He said: "Fuck! Where did you pick that up!" The CT scan revealed suspicious sightings in the soft tissue, near the spine, behind the kidneys, in the abdomen. Finally, my breathing got extremely difficult—the lymphoma was blocking the drainage of the pleura, the sack around my right lung, compressing and compromising my oxygen supply. Since the doctors did not know what I had, they treated me for the worst with the strongest possible dose of four types of chemotherapy and a new monoclonal antibody treatment, called *Mabthera*[2] in Israel. The whole package is code-named CHOP + R.

> The chemo is in an indiscriminate artillery barrage
> The Mabthera is a targeted assassination.
>
> Since my lymph is abnormal
> life has become abnormal
> I have crossed over
> into the village of the sick.
>
> She is not happy with my chest X-ray
> There are still 2 liters of fluid inside
> The fluid is thick, viscous, "loculated"
> Each day I receive a medical vocabulary lesson.
> *Loculated* means
> that the fluid is located in separated compartments
> like the Titanic.

2 In the United States it is known as *Rituxin* or *rituxamab*.

The Wounded Analyst

Today, there are no tests. I am not a patient today; instead I take care of my own patients. I make a mental note to construct an up-to-date patient list just in case—in the event of—my death—and suddenly I am sobbing for the first time since I heard, alone in the bathroom. I go to my office and make that list, preparing copies to give to colleagues in case sessions need to be canceled when I have chemo, or worse. The rest of the day, I sit and listen to other people. One lady, a senior mental health professional, recalls the brutal abuses of her father and then of the men in her life. She sobs, "I am damaged, so damaged." Later I want to transfer her to another analyst, but she cries again, saying, "Don't you understand, I cannot go to another analyst. I just cannot." Another patient, a young man, is about to be married. Every moment of joy brings the anguish of a missing father, murdered in a terrorist attack. He says he will never be happy again, not even on his wedding day. I am suddenly terrified that this will also be my children's fate.

> Towards evening, my breathing becomes even worse
>
> pain stalks each sitting position
>
> I do not know what to do with myself.
>
> For the first time, I feel
>
> really miserable.
>
> I cannot face another unslept night.

> I have my first scary dream:
>
> I am driving in a car with my wife in a city street.
>
> We are going down a gentle incline
>
> And I want to slow the car down
>
> But I cannot move my foot from pedal to brake
>
> Momentarily immobilized
>
> I cry out for help …

> Today my first MD introduces me to the lymphoma specialist
>
> who will be treating me.

I tell her my story.

How the lymphoma infiltrated the muscles that control eye movement.

How fluid accumulated in the lungs and showed small B-cells

CT: masses around my spine, reticular bodies, kidneys, neck, pelvis

But that most are clots

So that even the biopsy

they took out of my back may not be good enough for histo-diagnosis.

Hematologists love histology

and love to see both the individual cell

but also how the cells aggregate, the cellular architecture.

I say it sounds very Jungian,

You want to see the individual and the collective.

They say "Exactly."

I ask why the bone marrow did not give more information

and again the immunological system sounds like adolescent psychology.

In the bone marrow, lymphocytes behave because they are under close supervision;

once they are on their own, they run wild;

so bone marrow does not show how wayward they will become, unsupervised.

My spleen is now twice its regular size; my lungs accumulating more fluid.

They discuss again the eye and rule out the operation but say

we may need to rebiopsy.

I hear for the first time talk about taking out my spleen

Finally, they track down my subtype.

Its name so well reflects my liminal state:

Marginal zone.

I am in the margins, all right.

But the real shock comes

When I ask about staging.

Naively I had thought,

since there were no obvious lymph nodes

I might be in Stage I

or Stage II.

She hesitates and I know it is bad.

"Tell me straight—*dugri*"

I have been strong staring death down

But I am not prepared for

"Stage IV" and worse,

there is an infected lymph node hidden and inaccessible down below.

Living with Chemo

How will chemo hit me? Will I be able to go on working?

Ever since my first CHOP chemo

There have been sores in my mouth

Along the ridges, between the gums

An entire palate hid its shame behind the tongue

Eating anything with edges makes me edgy.

I think of the difference between curing and healing.

A thief breaks into your house, leaves a terrible mess

and steals your mother's bracelet.

Later, the thief is caught and the bracelet returned

you are cured of the "theft"

But not healed of the violation of your home.

I am becoming cured

but will my body home be healed, restored, purified, strengthened.

When I was undergoing treatment, every moment felt precious. There was no time to waste. I felt over and over again the key question of individuation: What am I here to do? What is my destiny? At the time, I was editing a special edition of the Jungian journal *Harvest* on Erich Neumann,[3] who died age 55, exactly my age. I felt that I had been paying too much attention to the needs of others and not enough to my own destiny, so that I too would die without doing what I was supposed to do. Neumann's tragedy accompanied me everywhere.

The Analyst Changes—Persona Vanishes

Physical changes are the most striking aspect of illness, hiding and revealing the persona.

"To be well is a hobby;

to be sick is a full time job."

One of the central experiences of illness is loss.

In English, the word for illness is *dis-ease*

The loss of ease—

the ease not to know

when your next treatment or blood test is coming.

The loss of ease that each sensation, pain, sweaty night,

each ache, does not signal another medical earthquake.

The loss of a future spreading out before you like a set table.

Above all, for every cancer person,

there is the loss of "my body as I knew it."

For me, the bodily change was not

weight loss, a half closed eye, a massively swollen spleen that stole sleep, or

even panicking white blood cells

but one day after chemo, touching my chin

to see my beard fall like fresh snow.

Since I was 19, I have had a beard.

---

3 *Harvest: International Journal for Jungian Studies*, 52(2), 2006.

No one in Israel had seen my naked face;

not my wife, my children, my students, or my patients.

People did not recognize me; I did not recognize myself.

I would look in the mirror and say, "Who stole my face?"

I would walk up to old friends and start speaking, only to be told,

"Excuse me, sir, who are you?"

"Who am I, indeed?" I was another Henry: Henry the Sick.

Around that time, the

hematology department sent an invitation for a workshop with the collage artist Hanoch Piven

and my innermost soul felt "*aha.*"

Here is a chance

to do something about my beard.

I came with a bearded friend.

He brought

pine needles from his garden

and I brought dried foodstuffs (rice, beans, lentils, nuts, chickpeas, mushrooms) and kitchen utensils (wooden knives and metal choppers).

Kitchens are places of transformations, of the Great Mother,

where the raw becomes cooked

something that can be eaten and digested.

Each of us recreated my missing beard.

Doing these collages helped me mourn my beard and all it represented:

my masculine identity, my link to Jewishness and my bearded ancestors, and

the "me" who was no more.[4]

Cancer takes away so much;

but it also gives:

opportunities to see the world,

not how we want it to be, but as it is.

---

4 The collages can be viewed at Hanoch Piven's website: http://www.pivenworld.com/ha-noch-piven-creativity-workshops.

"You Have to Decide"

A Jungian colleague, she of the unexpectedly fractured pelvis,

Comes to my oxygenated home.

She shares the wisdom of being a sick analyst.

"Dealing with patients,"

she says: "You have to decide

Who you can work with and who you want to put off.

You have to do it your way.

To take care of yourself first."

Which is hard

since as analysts, we are so focused on looking after the others.

"Telling patients about your illness

means that you have to feel comfortable with them asking,

'How you are?'

"Some patients surprised me.

My being weak, allowed them to grow strong."

Just as the wounded healer paradigm might predict.

Shabbat protected me

From the pain

Discomfort and tyranny of the body

I feel my spleen shrink

Laugh with friends unseen for ages

And

Write as if there is no tomorrow

But as we see the Sabbath queen off

I feel feverish

I wake in the wolfish hour

To feel my spleen expanded, painful

Abandoned to the blackness of another week.

I am told
To wait
To practice the prime patient virtue: patience
From the Sanskrit, *pati*, to wait, to suffer
I am getting expert at both.

We come early for the procedure
Done by three unfamiliar medicos
And I think how easily we place our bodies
In the hands of strangers

Strange hands enter my body
Will they contaminate my soul?

I hope that by Shabbat I will once again be under the wings of the Shechinah.

Two Hematology Psalms

My two hematologists were healers of Biblical proportions and to honor them, I wrote two poems:

In the beginning,
God created the lymph and lymphoma
And there was chaos,
and darkness over the face of the fluid.
Until the medication, blessed be, hovered over the interface.
God said: Let there be light! And there was light!
God saw the light through the microscope
and saw that the cells were good.
God separated the cells, the dark from the light.
He called the light, *lymph* and the darkness, *lymphoma*.
And from out of the coma, there was hope.

* * *

The hematologist is my shepherd

I shall not want.

She makes me lie down on green examining table

and renews my life

She guides me thru the right protocol

as befits my subtype.

Though I walk in the valley of the spleen

I shall not fear

she lays me down by the fluid

and comforts my nodules.

She guides me through the paths of bureaucracy

and shows me the power of imagery.

My blood brims over

and my chest is anointed with gel

Only monoclonal antibodies and chemotherapy shall pursue

all the days of my life.

my body shall dwell in the house of healing

all the years of my life.

Illness in the Analyst

In the end, the treatment was successful, and I left the village of the sick. I am now five years lymphoma-free. Clearly, I am one of the really lucky ones.

How has this experience changed me? When I was going through treatments and confronting mortality, I yearned for a spiritual breakthrough that would refocus my life. But it never came. I did decide to explore my inferior sensation function by learning to play saxophone and doing yoga and ceramic sculpture. But there was no great revelation. Rather, I gradually returned to doing what I had done previously but with more zest. Following his slow recovery from his heart attack, Jung wrote:

[s]omething else, too, came to me from my illness. I might formulate it as an affirmation of things as they are: an unconditional "yes" to that which is, without subjective protests—acceptance of the conditions of existence as I see them and understand them, acceptance of my own nature, as I happen to be.[5]

In a less dramatic fashion, as I left the village of the sick, I believe that I too accepted my own nature. Jungian psychology, with its emphasis on spirit and Self, often neglects the body, and my illness has taught me to be more attentive and kind and appreciative of it. Nadezhda Mandelstam, wife of the great Russian poet Osip, in her memorable memoir *Hope Against Hope*, describes how her husband was exiled and persecuted unto death by Stalinists. Despite all that, she described him as "endlessly *zhizneradostny*"—literally, "life glad." I believe my illness has shown me how to be *zhizneradostny.*

My illness had yet another impact. I became concerned with how illness and dying/death impact on the lives of analysts and their patients.[6] In my training the issue of the ill or disabled analyst never arose, and I felt like I was making it up as I went along. I began investigating the topic and found little Jungian material, except a moving piece by Pamela Power about how the death of her analyst had impacted her life and her own illness.[7] I started interviewing analysts who were sick and those who had recovered, as well as patients of deceased analysts, while giving writing seminars and workshops on the topic.[8] I now understand that it is crucial to confront our own illness and mortality *before* we get sick, otherwise the impact on the patients about whom we so care will be terrible. Ideally, patients of seriously ill or dying analysts ought to be transferred ahead of time.[9] Yet, I know from personal experience with dying colleagues and their analysands how difficult it was for them to let go of their patients, who provided them with so much vitality and meaning. Analysands often

---

5 C.G. Jung, *Memories, Dreams, Reflections*, p 328.

6 P. Dewald, "Serious illness in the analyst: Transference, countertransference and reality responses. "In *International Journal of Psychoanalysis, 30*(2), pp. 347–363; A.H. Kaplan & D. Rothberg, "The dying psychotherapist." *American Journal of Psychiatry, 143*, pp. 561–572; H. J. Schwartz, and A.L.S. Silver, eds. *Illness in the analyst: Implications for Treatment Relationship.*

7 P. Power, "Death of the analyst." *Journal of Jungian Theory and Practice, 7*(2), pp. 35–46.

8 H. Abramovitch, "Illness in the analyst." In *Facing multiplicity: Psyche nature culture.*

9 A.H. Kaplan & D. Rothberg, "The dying psychotherapist." *American Journal of Psychiatry, 143*, pp. 561–572.

complained bitterly that they had stayed in analysis only for the sake of their analyst, long after it ceased to be for their own needs. They also said how hard it was to start with someone else. The unexpected and unworked-through death of an analyst can have a profound and disturbing effect not only on analysands and candidates but on the entire analytical community.[10] I hope when my time comes to join my mother in the realm of the ancestors, I will have the courage to follow my own good advice.

I want to end with a poem by Osip Mandelstam that brings together the themes of death, resurrection, and joy in living:

> *Mounds of human heads are wandering into the distance.*
> *I dwindle among them. Nobody sees me. But in books*
> *much loved, and in children's games I shall rise*
> *from the dead to say the sun is shining.*[11]

---

10 R. Lasky, "Catastrophic illness in the analyst and the analyst's emotional reaction to it." *International Journal of Psychoanalysis, 71*, pp. 455–473; R. Fajardo, "Life-threatening illness in the analyst." *International Journal of Psychoanalysis, 49*(2), pp. 569–586.

11 Osip Mandelstam, "341" from THE SELECTED POEMS OF OSIP MANDELSTAM, p. 84, translated by Clarence Brown and W.S. Merwin. Translation copyright © 1973 by Clarence Brown and W.S. Merwin, used by permission of The Wylie Agency LLC.

References

Abramovitch, H. "Illness in the analyst." In *Facing multiplicity: Psyche nature culture,* ed. P. Bennett. Proceedings of the XVIIIth Congress of IAAP. Einsiedeln, Switzerland: Daimon Verlag, 2012.

Dewald, P. "Serious illness in the analyst: Transference, countertransference and reality responses. "In *International Journal of Psychoanalysis, 30*(2), 347–363, 1982.

Kaplan, A. H., and D. Rothberg. "The dying psychotherapist." *American Journal of Psychiatry, 143,* 561–572, 1986.

Fajardo, R. "Life-threatening illness in the analyst. *"International Journal of Psychoanalysis, 49*(2), 569–586, 2001.

Jung, C. G. *Memories, Dreams, Reflections,* Ed. Aniela. Jaffe. New York: Vintage Books, 1989.

Lasky, R. "Catastrophic illness in the analyst and the analyst's emotional reaction to it." *International Journal of Psychoanalysis, 71,* 455–473, 1990.

Levinson, D. *The Seasons of a Man's Life.* New York: Ballantine Books, 1986.

Mandelstam, N. *Hope Against Hope.* New York: Modern Library, 1999.

Mandelstam, O. "341" from THE SELECTED POEMS OF OSIP MANDELSTAM, translated by Clarence Brown and W.S. Merwin. Translation copyright © 1973 by Clarence Brown and W.S. Merwin, used by permission of The Wylie Agency LLC.

Power, P. J. "Death of the analyst." *Journal of Jungian Theory and Practice, 7*(2), 35–46, 2005.

Schwartz, H. J., and A. L. S. Silver, eds. *Illness in the analyst: Implications for Treatment Relationship.* Madison, CT: International Universities Press, 1990.

The Church of Her Body

by Sharon Heath

"Come, said my Soul,

Such verses for my Body let us write (for we are one) …" [1]

The year I entered the analytic training program at the C.G. Jung Institute of Los Angeles was marked by three other life-changing events. I was beset by the first of a series of physical ailments that would come to baffle me and what seemed like half the doctors in Los Angeles; I began writing my first novel; and a big dream appeared, announcing what would become the fierce arc of my life as an analyst. In that dream, a stranger led me across a bridge from a small apartment complex to a considerably larger one, where a door to an unfamiliar apartment awaited us, just slightly ajar. From the crack in the doorway, a blinding white light emanated, and a voice warned from inside, "Don't come any closer." The scene shifted to an open landscape, and I saw a line of women doing an undulating dance in unison, their arms making graceful wave motions, like reeds in the wind, like a hula. This scene was accompanied by a second voice that instructed me, "It will be your task to establish the Church of Her Body, as opposed to His Story." Little did I suspect at the time my dream would herald a descent into a dark night of the body that would equal and sometimes surpass the dark night of the soul that originally led me to Jung.

I knew a little about the hula. When I was five, I'd taken hula lessons with my mother, seguing on my own to ballet and then modern dance. But it was to the hula that psyche returned in my dream of the Church of Her Body, the dance I'd learned at the side of my personal mother, a flowing interconnection of woman to woman and woman to nature with the rocking of the hips and the seductive play of hands.

The pleasurable memory of dancing with my mother was particularly precious since my early home life—though warm and loving—had been stamped by wounding in both body and soul. As the sole child of her Russian-Jewish immigrant parents

---

1 Whitman, *Leaves of Grass.*

to survive beyond the age of five, my mother wasn't exactly at home in her body; she smoked like a chimney, decried her feminine roundness as ugly, and suffered tremendous anxiety, chronic illnesses, and dangerous accidents. My Ukraine-born father's first life memory was of hiding in tall rushes beside a river from men on horseback determined to kill any Jews they could find during an Easter-time pogrom; he struggled with a tragic sense of the cruelty and dangerousness of existence and took refuge in the life of the mind, railing at any hint of religion or irrationality.

My parents, brother, and I shared a large home with my maternal grandparents, two sets of aunts and uncles, and two cousins, and, by the time I was five, three of those people had died. One of them was my bubbie. She and my zayda had cared for me from my first months, as soon as my mother returned to full-time waitressing. I recall my bubbie as a striking woman, with a soft manner and luminous eyes; my zayda was a bull of a man, with an erect bearing and a walrus mustache. Zayda was given to chasing away kids he thought were hurting me, his Yiddish-accented voice a booming trumpet, and I was both embarrassed and relieved by his protectiveness. I was a physically fearful child.

While my grandparents brought an Old World solidity to my life, their terror that I would die cast a spell over me. I was, after all, the sole biological child of their sole surviving child. Their dead babies hovered over me like dark little clouds, dripping into me and penetrating my cells and muscles. Experiencing my body as precariously vulnerable and the world as dangerous, I went undercover, becoming a quiet, shy, and profoundly depressed child.

The Hermosa Beach community where we lived was populated at the time by Baptist Dust Bowl refugees, and their pale skinned, tow-headed children often called me "Nigger." In those days, we had garbage incinerators behind our houses; one time when I was playing alone in the alley, two older boys pushed me down onto the ground and forced ashes into my mouth. I felt ashamed to be dark and female and little, and didn't tell a soul. It was small wonder that I submerged my creative drive for years and was hesitant to play with other children. Instead, once my bubbie died, I kept my lonely zayda company for hours on end while we watched a sycamore outside our front window.

When, years later, I entered the Jung Institute training program, shame, fearfulness, and hiddenness walked in with me, along with courage, anticipation, and the strength of generations who'd managed to survive the worst. Within weeks of entering that initiatory passageway, I was stricken by a mysterious abdominal condition that felt like a burning sun at the center of my belly, a crying wound at my core.

As soon as I had my dream of the Church of Her Body, I set to work trying to discern its meaning. I was filled with questions like: "How might I think about this dream alchemically? Why was I instructed to back away from that bright light? And whose body was the dream referring to—the Great Goddess's, my mother's, my own?" Associating that blinding light to alchemical masculine energy, or *Sol*, I felt pretty confident in assuming I was being led away from my tendency to identify with my father's rationalism and in the direction of embodied feminine rhythms . . . but I had no idea what that would actually mean. My belly symptoms continued to heat up, and I found my energies pulled toward my own body, first and foremost. When nerves are sending off powerful signals, you pay attention. Amongst other things, I unearthed the resentment of a child who'd tamped down her own vital energies out of fear of dying … and living. I sank into a state of helplessness, bathed in a muddy bath of shame, imagined an angry patriarchal god—the Adonai my atheistic parents had rejected—punishing me for everything creepy or weak about me.

Over time, more painful syndromes slid in for the ride: fibromyalgia, chronic fatigue, paresthesia, interstitial cystitis, burning mouth. Most of the symptoms evoked burning imagery; I felt stuck in a permanent *calcinatio*, a state of unrelenting self-incubation.

Desperate for palliation, if not cure, I *shlepped* without much result from one mainstream or holistic doctor to another. At the same time, I was subtly aware that my suffering was cooking me. On one level, I was feeling tortured by pain, exhaustion, a sense of entrapment in my body, rage at my fate, a fear of never getting relief. But I was also discovering a strength in myself I hadn't imagined. Nowhere was that more apparent than in my increasing engagement with writing. Poet May Sarton's remarkable poem *The Invocation to Kali* includes the lines:

> I am the cage where poetry
>
> Paces and roars. The beast
>
> Is the god. How murder the god?
>
> How live with the terrible god?[2]

2 Sarton, "The Invocation to Kali," *A Grain of Mustard Seed: New Poems.*

Pacing and roaring with my creative *daemon* helped me live with *my* terrible god. Little by little, I developed as a writer—my psyche demanding I work hard at the craft of fiction-writing in a parallel process with the fire of analytic training. Writing was my secret joy, deliciously selfish, an astonishing door into a world where a child who hadn't had much of a childhood could finally play. I was stunned that characters actually came to lives of their own as I put pen to the page.

A diagnosis of breast cancer heated things up even more. The cancer hit like a bolt out of the blue, discovered by a disbelieving radiologist in a routine mammogram. I met for the first time with my new oncologist to discuss treatment options on my fifty-third birthday.

I found myself making a personal commitment to combat any internal voices that wished me dead. I'd worked for years on my harsh inner critic. Now I found myself visualizing my inner attacker as a bully coming up a set of school steps to beat me up. I vowed to kick him back down the stairs each time he came after me. I was sobered to discover that I was having to kick him down thousands of times a day, but what was ultimately born of those repetitive efforts were the first glimmers of a more deeply rooted self-love.

My relationships—the feminine principle of relatedness—assumed a greater part of my consciousness. One of my friends told me, "I will not let you die." She knew—and I knew—that she didn't literally have such power, but the visceral vehemence of her commitment to me was profoundly fortifying. I cannot tell you how fully my body relaxed into those words. Another friend suggested I re-think the cold, if brilliant, oncologist I was thinking of going with, offering a referral to an entirely different sort of doctor.

In my novel *The Cut*, I offer a fictionalized version of my first encounter with my new doctor when the protagonist Evvie Kerr comes to the office of her oncologist, Dr. Moskowitz:

> You certainly couldn't accuse David Moskowitz of running a slick operation. His waiting room was circa 1970, the chairs some kind of ersatz leather, each of them scooped by thousands of seated asses into a kind of bowl shape that made you feel like you were perched directly on your tail bone. In one corner resided a dusty fish bowl, whose two salmon-and-cream-speckled inhabitants traced an incessant infinity sign above a few sprouts of fake greenery and a couple of plastic deep-sea divers probing the bottom of the bowl.

But David Moskowitz was a *mensch*. She got her first clue to that one when the short, salt-and-pepper mustached man, dressed in slightly rumpled slacks and a plaid flannel shirt, opened the door himself to the waiting room and called out her name.

She got her second when, ushering her into his consulting room, he pulled his chair around from behind his desk to sit closely facing her, cocking his head with genuine interest as he said, "So, how are you? I would imagine you're scared shitless, but I want you to know that, if this does turn out to be cancer, we have a whole host of treatments available that we didn't have even five years ago. And they're good. But, I'd imagine that's faint comfort to you right now."

Her third clue had come when, looking up toward the ceiling to try to coalesce some of the four million questions she wanted to ask him, she saw two cheaply-framed black and white photographs tilting haphazardly above his various diplomas. One was a shot of a bashfully grinning Bobby Kennedy, his sleeves rolled up to his elbows, reaching down to shake hands with migrant workers from the bed of a truck; the other showed Martin Luther King, Jr. facing the camera with such simple serenity that you just knew he'd already been to the mountaintop.

She'd breathed deeply, leaned forward, and began to tell her new oncologist exactly how crappy she felt.

Crappy *was* a pretty good description of how I felt. Mostly, I was dazed and overwhelmed, beset with creepy, crawly skin symptoms that had begun with the onset of peri-menopause and now were exacerbated by being yanked off estrogen cold-turkey. My "itchies," as I called them, would persist 24 hours a day throughout my several month radiation therapy and for some time afterwards.

If I'd had to tolerate unwelcome physical symptoms before cancer, feeling like I had ants ceaselessly crawling all over me as I continued to see patients and desperately needed a good night's sleep was more than I could bear. Every night, I'd settle into bed—a cat and a book at my side—hoping against hope I'd be able to sleep. But sleep was not to be.

With the amping up of my fibromyalgia and itchies, I felt stretched to my limits. That was when She came to me … not in dreams, because I wasn't able to sleep, but in nightly waking visions, a glorious presence in my bedroom. She was larger than life, about eight or ten feet tall, voluptuous, naked and dark-skinned, with long, wavy black hair coiling down Her strong shoulders. She was on all fours, moving on hands and knees, and I was a child, clinging to Her midsection, hands clasped round Her back, like a baby possum. Each night during my seven weeks of radiation therapy, She inched the two of us a little further through a dense jungle. In just that way, She saved my life. I called Her Eve.

She became my inner muse, as well as the centerpiece of my second novel, *Zero Visibility*. I began the novel during cancer treatment and was quite aware my creative efforts represented a healing lifeline. I wrote in the midst of pain, itching, and exhaustion—urged on by the ineluctable demand that a story be told.

The story was that of a lost young mail carrier, Ariel Thompkins, whose spiritual hunger comes to consciousness when she learns that the world's oldest human fossil is being brought to U.C.L.A.'s Fowler Museum. In the following scene, Ariel has fallen asleep on the couch next to her cat Jezebel. She wakens to a flashing TV screen:

> She yanked the laundry basket at her feet up onto the couch and began to fold carelessly, when tonight's current specimen announced an upcoming news bit about "'First Eve,'" after a few words from our sponsor."
>
> "Not our sponsor," she objected to Jezebel—who looked up from a serious hind leg licking, as if to agree.
>
> When the anchorman's face came back up on the screen, she could hardly believe the smug substitute for wit with which he described "the return of Eve to our own Garden of Eden," in front of a crude rendering of a flat-nosed, toothless crone, depicting what the anthropological find might have looked like when blood coursed around her now denuded bones.
>
> "Let's hope this baby'll get herself some plastic surgery while she's visiting," the jerk yukked to his female co-anchor, who grinned fatuously back at him before moving right on to "the fabulous weather Eve can expect to greet her when she arrives at U.C.L.A."
>
> "That's it?" Ariel shouted at the screen. "The ancestress of all of us gets discovered, and all you can say is that she needs a nose job?"
>
> She cradled her knees with her arms. She wanted more, wished they'd kept the drawing of Eve up on the screen so she could look into the rendering of those ancient black eyes. She imagined them looking back at her in recognition. Rubbing her hands down her own thighs and shins, Ariel wanted to stroke those old bones into life again.

As I tackled this scene, Eve took me back to my own adolescent struggle to find a way to connect with the changes in my body. If the personal mother has been unable to model and mediate a celebration of transmutation from girl body to woman body, fertile body to crone, the sacred round of death and rebirth can only be experienced as demonic.

Which had been pretty much the state of my own god image when my physical symptoms first began. Only after completing my fourth novel did it dawn on me that each novel I worked on had moved my experience of the numinosity of the body from something initially dark and persecutory in the direction of imagery and affect that were increasingly expansive and open-ended.

I was aware from the beginning that the title I'd given my fourth novel suggested an urge to bring together the images of His Story and the Church of Her Body from my big dream. Like every creative work, the novel soon developed a life of its own that confounded, stretched, and transcended the ego hard at work on it.

The History of My Body ended up being a first-person narrative of young Fleur Robins, a unique child who some might call autistic, others might describe as a savant, and still others might see as just-who-she-is. I named the protagonist Fleur because *flower* had been the first word I'd spoken as a child. I found myself having to run to catch up with all she wanted to teach me.

Fleur is born on the expansive estate of her abusive, anti-abortionist senator father and his considerably younger alcoholic wife. Her grandfather has lived with them ever since he was rendered mute by a stroke. A whole wing of their house is devoted to care of children whom Senator Robins fosters. The babies are clothed in what Fleur calls "Martian infant sacks," since the baby pajamas have arms, but no feet. The family is served by an odd staff of spinsters, including a housekeeper, Fayga, a nanny with all the finesse of a Mack truck, and her mother's companion, who happens to be an ex-nun. Fleur is beset with fears of the void; it is her frame of reference, her torment, and ultimately the key to her transformation.

In the following scene, Fleur describes running to her Grandfather after an uncomfortable experience with her cat Jillily:

> I tried to tell myself that it would never have happened if she hadn't gotten taken to the vet to get fixed. Personally, I had no idea why she had to get fixed. I never noticed anything about Jillily that looked broken. To me, she was perfect in every way. But in the weeks after coming back from the vet, she walked funny, her white furry belly all loose and hangy and swaying from side to side. I figured anything that pouchy-looking was fair game for a pinch, so one day when I came into my bedroom and she

was lying on her back on a little patch of sun on the carpet the way she likes to do, with her legs spread open and her paws flapped up in the air, I felt the itching for a pinch come over me, the way it can. Everybody laughed at Jillily when she struck that particular pose of hers. Fayga would call her Charlotte the Harlot, but then Sister Flatulencia would make a mean squint of her flying saucer eyes and Nana would say, "Hush!"

Anyway, there was Jillily, my favorite person in the whole world besides my grandfather, even though Nana has always insisted that Jillily isn't really a person. Sometimes Nana's mind is just a little limited, if you know what I mean. But Nana wasn't there when I reached down and gave that empty-looking belly a nice, squeezy pinch. In one quick second, the world went black as the blankest void. Jillily yowled and gave me a look like I'd sold her to the devil abortionists, then she ran away from me and squatted under my four-poster, with her body clenched up all tight and the muscles in her back twitching like she was being bitten by fleas. I flattened myself like a crocodile to slither under the bed and coax her back out, and I had to give her a thousand chicken-peck kisses all over her back and ears and belly before she let her motor whirr again, and when she finally let me kiss her little pink triangle of a nose, I could see the wet gook in the corners of her yellow eyes and I knew that I'd made Jillily cry.

That was my first time realizing there are some things worse than boredom. My whole body felt like something ugly and stinky and I kept wishing that my skin was a pair of pajamas I could just take off and fling into Fayga's dirty clothes bin, along with all those Martian infant sacks. A part of me wanted to bite off my ugly, stinking fingers, but Jillily's whirring told me she needed me to keep patting her, so I kept my fingers out of my mouth and stroked Jillily with them, instead.

That afternoon, I told Grandfather what I'd done. We were sitting together facing the big lead-paned front window of Grandfather's bedroom, Grandfather in his recliner and me in my giant-sized, cushiony rocking chair that I'd inherited from my mother. We were watching our tree like we always did, and I kept opening my mouth to say what was on my mind and then closing it again. It was only after the last mockingbird had flown away and the branches looked as desolate as a motherless baby that I finally turned to Grandfather and told him. For a long time, he looked at me, his eyes brimming over with kindness, and then he stretched out his big, twisty hand and put it over my evil, Jillily-pinching one and he made his sounds."[3]

Writing about Fleur had the effect on me of liberating a newfound playfulness. Much to my chagrin, she insisted on becoming a quantum physicist, forcing me—who never got beyond physiology in high school—to try to stretch my brain to con-

3 Heath, *The History of My Body*.

template the most basic of concepts in that mind-boggling field. In the novel, Fleur makes a significant scientific breakthrough, thanks, in part, to learning about the Hindu image of Indra's Web. The imagery of the heaven of the god Indra—comprised of a vast, criss-crossing net, with jewels suspended from each intersection mirroring every other jewel in the web—seems to be coming into its own in our current era—with the Internet and World Wide Web echoing its very name and global ecological consciousness echoing its spirit.

Unbeknownst to me at the time, through my suffering and my writing, I'd been working my way from a punitive patriarchal god image to a primordial great goddess to the *unus mundus* of an interconnected web linking human to human, human to animal, planet, and cosmos in one endless, interwoven dance. I saw a living amplification of that concept just last year, as I watched a huge cluster of bees break off from its overcrowded nest in my backyard in a bee version of cell division and begin to move to a new location. It moved as a single unit. In fact, watching it, I thought I was observing a hard, oval structure rather than a vibrating living organism, its individual bees moving together as one.

I know now that my body has its own part in that extraordinary natural scheme. On January 23, 2010, I suffered a bout of sleeplessness, occasioned by a rare recurrence of fibromyalgia. What came to me in my pain was an image of Mother Earth trying to decide whether to continue to be patient with us marauding, despoiling humans or just shake us off her body in disgust. I finally fell asleep in the wee hours of the morning, only to wake to news of Haiti's massive quake. How much, I wondered, of my body's pain has been my own share of the earth's suffering? How much of my physical distress has been a kind of *solastalgia,* a manifestation the pain we experience when our home environment is threatened?

Like it or not, my God keeps speaking to me. These days, I am more likely to look at my bodily symptoms as expressing, not only sensitivity to environmental toxins, a conflict between the impulse to hide and an urge to express, and a cellular and muscular organization around early trauma, but also the death by fire of one of my mother's siblings, goddess-worshipping women wearing Scold's bridles and being burnt at the stake, our Mother planet heating up in crisis, and alchemical transformation at work—with the *daemon* of my creativity insisting that my ego continually submit to new incarnations clamoring to be born.

Ariel Thompkins, Evvie Kerr, Fleur Robins, and protagonists yet to come would not exist but for my physical suffering. My holy affliction is the fertilizer for their creation. Between the archetypal poles of affect and image is the body itself. Like the earth from which she is formed, she is bountiful, real, finite, implacable … and she keeps aiming me toward opening new doors, coming out of hiding, catching a gift or two and paying forward the wonderful, terrible beauty of being alive.

References

Heath, Sharon. *The History of My Body*. Carmel, CA: Genoa House, 2011.

Sarton, May. *A Grain of Mustard Seed: New Poems*. New York and London: W.W. Norton & Company, 1971.

Whitman, Walt. *Leaves of Grass*. New York: Modern Library, Following the Arrangement of the Edition of 1891–2.

Section Five
Writing the Fire

*I always knew he must be able to write the fire he can speak—and here
it is. His published books are doctored up for the world at large, or rather
they are written out of his head and this out of his heart.*

—Carey Baynes, Introduction to *The Red Book*

A Truchas story: It is the evening of the Day of the Dead and the four of us are invoking our ancestors. I tell about a relative of mine, Illinois poet Vachel Lindsay from the early 20ᵗʰ century. My family has many of his old papers. They speak of him as crazy. Perhaps this is because he committed suicide. Perhaps it is because of his exuberant chanting of his poems, not unlike Alan Ginsberg or Dylan Thomas. Oh, that Midwestern reserve! Dan Googles "Vachel Lindsay," and we learn that Lindsay was a social and environmental activist and his poetry was the medium of his message.

Spending the evening with this distant relative of mine, we also learn he was one of the first "sung" poets, his art compelling and controversial. One of his more famous poems, "The Congo," was declared racial stereotyping even then, which he adamantly denied. In later years he felt constricted by the popularity of his dramatic performances, declaring, "I will not be a parrot of myself!" I gained empathy for this man, knowing the courage it takes to be so open with one's soul. It is a dark side of the creative, one with which all writers have to grapple. P.D.

Dennis Patrick Slattery: *The Soul's Claim: Choose It or Lose It*

Robert D. Romanyshyn: *I Only Ever Wanted to be a Bus Driver:*
An Unfinished Life

Naomi Ruth Lowinsky: *Drunk with Fire: How The Red Book Transformed My Jung*

Dennis Slattery, Robert Romanyshyn, and Naomi Ruth Lowinsky all tell of their struggles to make room for the poet. Slattery wrestled with mainstream academic psychology. Romanyshyn was torn between two intense callings: philosophy and poetry.

Lowinsky works out her breach with Jung, who was suspicious of artists. She engages Jung in active imagination. They become drinking buddies by the primordial fire.

The Soul's Claim
Choose it or Lose It

by Dennis Patrick Slattery, Ph.D.

I was guided to a general interest in psychology and then (by divine grace) to C.G. Jung's work through my father's alcoholism. When I was 16, I could not understand how my father, drunk on a Saturday night and in a full-blown rage, could begin shouting as I came home after a twelve-hour shift at the supermarket: "You are useless, no good, a waste!" How could I be useless? I had paid for my own tuition at a private high school, I bought my own cars as soon as I could drive, and I provided my father with bus fare with my earnings. What else could I possibly do to win his approval? I did not know at the time what projection was or what demons laid just below the surface of respectability, ready to uncoil each weekend in a drunken rage. So I began to search for answers. Beginning at a community college in downtown Cleveland, Ohio, I enrolled in as many psychology courses as I could fit into my full schedule. This was my tentative initiation into the study of soul.

In these classes I sought answers to my deeply embedded wound: in the face of all of my successes and achievements, I was still dubbed Sir Worthless. However, the psychology classes I enrolled in were too embedded in the world of "knee-jerks, myna birds, and rats," as the best of my professors, Blake Crider, a practicing analyst in Cleveland, called the clinical perspective of the day. He taught Abnormal Psychology of Everyday Life, and there I began to learn of the imagination behind the words of my alcoholic father. I was drawn to the word "abnormal" like a moth to the flame. "This has relevance to my life," I remember admitting one day after class. I began at the same time to discern that there were *schools* of psychology, although the degree program I entered as a psychology major at Kent State University in the mid-1960s relied heavily on experimental psychology. But I also began pursuing a double major and enrolled in upper-division literature and poetry courses. I soon realized that there is more psychology on any page of Fyodor Dostoevsky's *Crime and Punishment* or Malcolm Lowry's *Under the Volcano* or Graham Greene's *The Power and the Glory* than in a chapter (or even an entire textbook) of experimental psychology theory and practice. For me, knee-jerks and rats were displaced by the mind of a murderer and the lost faith of a whiskey priest. These images I could live with.

Although I was delighted with literary studies and the nuanced expressions of poetry, I was still disappointed with what psychology delivered as the voice of the soul. Disappointment gave way quickly to delight, however, when a graduate student in comparative literature at Kent State befriended me and encouraged me to read a book he had recently discovered: C.G. Jung's *Modern Man in Search of a Soul*.[1] This was in 1967. I still have that reprint of the original black paperback copy, published by Harcourt, Brace & World, with what looks like a galaxy or an atom spinning about it; it sits by my side as I type these words. If a work other than scripture can be called a spiritual guide, then Jung's book was my new lodestar for both spiritual and psychological awakening. A life can turn in a new direction as quickly as a chapter of a book emphatically grips one's interest and changes the trajectory of one's life.

I turn its pages now and see the red underlining I did so neatly with a ruler and the marginal notes in my scrawling, choppy 23-year-old handwriting. I can still feel the excitement in those scrawls, which I made hastily, wanting to move on to the next page, the next discovery, the impending idea, the further insight that would make my stomach grumble, roil, and rejoice in new insights.

What did I feel was important enough to mark in bright red? In the chapter "The Aims of Psychotherapy," Jung wrote:

> About a third of my patients are suffering from no clinically definable neurosis, but from the senselessness and emptiness of their lives.[2]

In a later chapter, "The Stages of Life," Jung discusses the place of the intellect in daily matters, and then observes:

> But beyond that there is a thinking in primordial images—in symbols which are older than historical man; what have been ingrained in him from earliest times, and, eternally living, outlasting all generations, still make up the groundwork of the human psyche.[3]

---

1 Jung, *Modern Man in Search of a Soul*.
2 Jung, *Modern Man in Search of a Soul*, 61.
3 Jung, *Modern Man in Search of a Soul*, 112–113.

Finally, a third revelation moved me so much that I wrote in red at the top of the page "Reread" and next to the passage a star and "Know":

> Sensation establishes what is actually given, thinking enables us to recognize its meaning, feeling tells us its value, and finally intuition points to the possibilities of the whence and whether that lie within the immediate facts.[4]

I was spellbound by these four functions that can orient us in the world; they revealed psychological writing that represented and reflected something tangible in my interior life that I no longer had to think of as mine alone. I was part of a universal psychological order that was ancient, accessible, and worthy of further development. Psychology and poetry began to meld into one vision of human life in these passages, which I absorbed like a starving soul seeking sustenance.

I immediately ceased my pursuit of experimental psychology courses at Kent State and began to devote much of my spare time to reading Jung's work, rereading his descriptions of the personal and collective unconscious, anima energy, shadow qualities of the soul, and the hunger for purpose in life, and I felt all of humanity begin to wrap around me. I was in a chrysalis of my own self-discovery. Here was a psychologist, I realized, who was more in touch with the labyrinth of my life than with laboratory experiments with rhesus monkeys and albino rats. But the biggest surprise was still waiting in the wings. It arrived in the form of another essay in the book that yoked depth psychology and poetry in new and exciting ways.

The Poetic Psyche

In this small paperback that was changing my interests, my perspective, and my life's study in big ways was an essay that intrigued me with its title: "Psychology and Literature." Its coupling of the two disciplines that attracted me the most infused hope into my grand design, hope that the poetic imagination might indeed have collegial, even intimate conversations with the psyche as Jung had defined it for me. The timing was extraordinary, for at this time in my undergraduate career I had joined the staff of the literary magazine *The Kent Quarterly* and was just beginning, with the encouragement of a creative writing teacher, Barbara Child, to write and submit poetry. I felt a certain shame about her pushing me, for to go public with such private utterances was

---

4 Jung, *Modern Man in Search of a Soul*, 93.

to step boldly outside what I had allowed myself before. I did not know what I was doing, but the call to express myself in a medium that I loved to read would neither dissipate nor decline. Jung's thinking, in fact, provided further energy to this new phase of expression. I tracked this essay that was so seminal for my own thinking back to its original publication in *The Spirit in Man, Art, and Literature,* Volume 15 of the *Collected Works of C.G. Jung.*[5]

What excited me about the essays in *The Spirit in Man, Art, and Literature?* I think it was that Jung offered a kind of language that was at once intuitive, personal, and universal. His prose carried both individual import and timeless significance, in part because he so often addressed and amplified the meaning inherent in the myth of a person's life. I found myself elated by Jung's observation that "it is obvious enough that psychology, being a study of psychic processes, can be brought to bear on the study of literature, for the human psyche is the womb of all the arts and sciences."[6] Two issues sprang at me from his observation: the idea that the psyche has ancient processes and patterns within its being that continue to recur, and the idea that the psyche is a womb, a metaphor that gave it a power as the genesis of all the creative work one engages. His language itself was poetic! He thought, at least here, like a poet and an explorer. No other psychologist or theorist in my experience thought like that at the time, except for Rollo May, who also used literature to great effect in his study of human behavior. But May's work was not to influence me until several years later with his publication of *Love and Will.*[7]

Jung's attitude toward creativity and the soul encouraged me to submit two poems to *The Kent Quarterly* in my junior year. Both were accepted. I share my first publication here. It tells the story of something I witnessed in a restaurant close to the boarding house off campus where I had a room. Harry, another boarder in the same house, was blind. In spite of this formidable obstacle, he was pursuing a master's degree in sociology. He and I had became good friends, and at times I would read his textbooks to him as part of a government program to assist blind college students.

---

5 Jung, *The Spirit in Man, Art, and Literature. CW15.* This thinnest volume of the *Collected Works* was to assume enormous formative power in helping me bridge the poetic landscape and the psyche.
6 Jung, *CW15,* ¶. 133.
7 May, *Love and Will.*

What I witnessed through the window of the coffee shop was Harry at the counter having a cup of soup while three coeds sitting at a table watched him and mocked his gestures. The event infuriated me. I entered the shop, approached Harry, and began a conversation with him, which dampened the spirits of the three young women, who soon left. That night I composed this poem:

Darkness

Is the third day
When leaves are waterlogged,
Crushed without a sound,
And a blind boy in a noisy
Smoke and grease-filled
Restaurant sits and eats alone;
Opening his mouth wide so as
Not to miss the soup-filled
Spoon as
Drops of rain drip off his
Forehead and arrogant
Bastardly coeds look
On and laugh.[8]

This poem was important to write because it both eased the anger I felt and made a *public statement* of it for others. But more than that: something happened to me in the experience of transforming an event into clumsy verse. Through the poem, I began to see the world differently, in a way that was simultaneously intimate and detached. Writing the poem deepened my consciousness of an event that lasted only minutes. The event, I recalled later, was analogous to what happens to the bitter and lost young man Ishmael in Melville's *Moby-Dick* when he befriends a tattooed islander at Peter Coffin's inn early in the novel.[9] Queequeg is holding a book that he cannot read, although he is perfectly content to count the pages. In the presence of this otherly person, Ishmael becomes aware of a strange sensation, as if something is melting in

---

8 Slattery, *Casting the Shadows: Selected Poems*, ix.
9 Melville, *Moby-Dick*.

him, some feeling of his bitterness and anger dissolving. I felt a similar dissolution of the anger I first experienced when I watched the college girls mocking Harry in the restaurant. Through crafting the poem, I had entered another realm, one that was larger and yet very particular in its structure—the landscape of the poetic image within the larger landscape of the imagination as a way of knowing. I had, however imperfectly, given a form to what would have, over time, faded into the forgotten past. Writing had retrieved it for future contemplation.

Images were the keys to the experience to be conveyed. The poetic images of the rainy day, the waterlogged leaves, the greasy air of the restaurant, Harry's blindness, and the soup he was enjoying were ways for me to organize experience along a different pathway in the embodied psyche, where emotion and intellect as well as the sensate world could commingle to create a new shape to that experience. The images are mindful ways of gathering an emotion into a bundle and then allowing the emotion to inform the image, even *be* the image. The images I used in the poem were equivalences, even emotional analogues of my soul's response to what I witnessed; they served to fix the experience, even to ritualize it into a meaningful whole. All of this I found exhilarating and immensely satisfying.

This experience was a kind of poetic expression that derived from my conscious experience, what Jung would call a psychological rather than a visionary experience. The former, he observes, is drawn "from man's conscious life," yet it is transformed by the poet, "raised from the commonplace to the level of poetic experience and expressed with a power of making us vividly aware of those everyday happenings which we tend to evade or to overlook because we perceive them only dully or with a feeling of discomfort."[10] I remember considering that poetry can be a rendering in verse of a human experience that perhaps, through the use of figures of speech and action, can raise the poet as well as the reader to a higher level of consciousness by giving shape and form to what one has perceived. Suddenly the mystery of poetry, although it was by no means negated or diminished, was placed into a category of awareness that I could comprehend. Poetry's ability to charm was enhanced by Jung's perception.

But what was so provocative was how Jung took the process deeper—down, in, and through the mystery of the psyche in its poetic mode of utterance and understanding. From him I learned that many of the images, fantasies, and dreams I thought were

---

10 Jung, *CW15*, , ¶139.

mine were part of a larger psychic whole, that I was not necessarily personally "responsible" for them, that they had a life force of their own. He revealed this powerful insight to me in these words:

> It is strange that a deep darkness surrounds the sources of the visionary material. This is the exact opposite of what we find in the psychological mode of creation, and we are led to suspect that this obscurity is not unintentional."[11]

I felt a fierce freedom in me attend this observation. Images that rose up in me from my reading or as a result of an experience from the day or a fantasy that suddenly abrupted itself into my consciousness or a film that I dreamt about on subsequent nights after seeing it—all these were not self-manufactured but arose from a deeper layer of being, one that was more collective and impersonal. Jung asked:

> What if there were a living agency beyond our everyday human world—something even more purposeful than electrons? Do we delude ourselves in thinking that we possess and control our own psyches, and is what science calls the "psyche" not just a question-mark arbitrarily confined within the skull, but rather a door that opens upon the human world from a world beyond?[12]

These questions provoked further speculation in me. Some mysterious otherness attended my waking and dreaming consciousness that I could neither be blamed nor praised for. The feeling of this mystery, far from frightening me, made me want to invite it in. I began to rise at 4 a.m. seven days a week so I could attend to this new project.

I began to practice a ritual in my study: Each morning, I lit a candle and burned a stick of incense. When I was writing, I often played classical music or Gregorian chants in the background. The space of my work changed dramatically, as if I had just made room for something that in the past I had not even recognized existed. And just as dreams can evoke other dreams, I learned that poetry can provoke poetic responses. I began to write more poetry on a regular basis, now with the conviction that parts of my personal myth and the larger cultural myth I was embedded in and an even larger ancestral history that I was a direct descendant of were at play in creation. My emotional response was a feeling of liberation. I recognized for the first time two images

11 Jung, *CW15*, ¶ 144.
12 Jung, *The Spirit in Man, Art, and Literature*, ¶ 148.

working in me: midwife and conduit. Jung's thought opened me to the reality that I was as much a disciple of history as an inhabitant and at times a creator of it, that what formed in me was not my possession but something that was using me to reveal itself. Let me offer part of a poem to illustrate what I mean.

One morning in the early darkness of the day, I was in my study musing in my journal, which I write in each day for twenty minutes. In this meditation I pause to recollect the day before in order to invite yesterday to shake hands with the not-yet-today. I was reading poetry and thinking about what kind of knowledge poetic utterance provides the soul even as it emanates from that same source. The following was given in a voice that I trusted. It was not my voice but came from somewhere else.

Morning Muse in the Kitchen

Making poetry of pots and spoons
a dactyl of dishes
and sonnets—sunny side up
or a new scrambled rhyme scheme
that leaves no stains on the glasses
no water spots of distraction
that can enter as burnt toast
or jelly under the finger nail
that irritates a couplet into
an entire chaos of rhyme.

She patters bare feet here and there
across the red rug looking for
a spatula to turn the eggs
easy over into the light of an inspired
Instant
where everything can be seen without
the mist of coffee steam or
the hard cloud of prose.

Musing over the morning paper

the kitchen goddess remembers
every item cooking in the fridge
the ice cream hardening into stiff
quatrains that will not melt
in prosaic patterns of heat
in late afternoon.

She dries the dishes in pure
sunlight, orders their stacks
and steps out and back
and down to the Guadalupe
River for a morning memory
of her mother gliding past in
a tube atop a shallow current
full of silent promise laid out
in neat Petrarchan echoes.

From the shore's rushes
birds of a certain genre
find comic relief in
labor pangs of free verse.[13]

Producing this poem was provocative for me because of its intention to find analogies of itself in metaphors that provide bridges to other, deeper realms like vertical stepping stones. I remember Jung's sense of the creative process that yokes levels of our realities to create something new, a delightful knowing in many cases: "Through our senses we experience the known, but our intuitions point to things that are unknown and hidden, that by their very nature are secret."[14] Each of us, he seems to suggest, carries within ourselves a secret life that art is often the best conduit for uncovering. Aspects of this secret life are ancient, inherited, re-membered and re-visioned anew, as with a living, organic mythos.

---

13 Slattery and Paris, *The Beauty between Words: Selected Poems,* 94–95.
14 Jung, *CW15,* ¶ 148.

Poetic responses are for me a large aperture into this realm. I trust this realm to reveal itself in the day's early hours, much like the angel Gabriel visiting the Virgin Mary during a time of quiet meditation when, as most paintings depict her, she is reading a book, engaged in the imagination and in a meditative open and porous position, fertile for revelation, open to intuitive intrusions. This image of the Annunciation, which has been depicted in hundreds of years of renderings, is the perfect psychic condition of repose for receiving a revelation. I attempted one morning to give voice to this experience in a poem:

Every Word Recalls Its Silence

Every word recalls its own silence.
Poetic words glaze
a keener memory. When uttered they
coax the strongest memories
of all. Each speech an act of remembrance;
each poetic musing marries a mythic past.
If I were to utter "Beatitude," say, would
the power shift in the East for an instant
so the meek might feel what it would be like
to inherit the earth?
And if I were to say "Beatrice,"
would she suddenly emerge to place
a token into the subway turnstile and
ride along the window into
underworld darkness?
A token gesture? A strength in even
An awkward motion to slake thirst?

I find the word "Beatific" memorable
on a grand scale for what in the heart
flutters when I utter it.
Darkness descends on every word—a divine

darkness that carries the dust of words
at Dusk—

Solitude seems indifferent, like desert's
right to ignore any footprint that breaks
the silence of sand and stone and
gray-green sage—ocotillo and saguaro,
wonderful sounds beneath desert
silence.

Memories play off darkness
hedging against the light. Silence glows
with a natural blush against the word
"Incarnate."
Silence surrounds Him like a shroud
cloaking the silent skin of the Incarnate
Word with a linen as white as it is breathless.

No soul might ever again clash with
such a splintered reflection. The eye
of Beatrice is a glass of silent memory
in a splash of subdued inflection.[15]

The images are given, consoling offerings to me for consideration. Not my imagination alone but another source, one that is psychic, ancient, and benevolent, presents these images to be arranged in some conscious crafted way to charm the felt sense of whatever marriage exists between words and silence. Because the process is a mystery, I make no attempts to explain it. But Jung continues to help me comprehend what the source or origin of such utterances might be. In part, what "appears in the vision is the imagery of the collective unconscious. This is the matrix of consciousness and has its own inborn structure.... Mythological motifs frequently appear, but clothed

---

15 Slattery, *Just below the Water Line: Selected Poems*, 64–65.

in modern dress; for instance, instead of the eagle of Zeus, or the great roc, there is an airplane; the fight with the dragon is a railway smash."[16]

What I hope I have elucidated here is the power of analogy that Jung's examples of mythic motifs gather to themselves. One level of reality or image or narrative seems to have a propensity toward likeness, correspondence, and affectionate accord with another. I venture to say that this is at the heart of the myth-making faculty of the psyche, and it takes on its most colorful garments in the form of stories, be they poetry or prose. My own creative process begins with trust, moves to porosity, and concludes with the making of something into a coherent, formed sense that can be shared. The end result is joy.

This last emotion is why I write, for the process itself is a therapy of the word. A haiku might make this observation more palpable:

Wounding

Harsh words attack him;

A friend grows angry with me.

I cannot unspeak.[17]

The haiku remembers something essential about the wound in the words we use. It offers it a new shape, a new reflection, one that, I hope, confers a moment of meditation and perhaps a scent of grace to the moment. It forms an experience into a recollection that is new. It also carries the duality that I will end this essay with by quoting from the rich lode of Jung's writings. For readers new to Jung's work, I will offer this: a little Jung goes a long way. By this I mean that he constantly invites us to meditate on what he observes. Often his observations in prose are as tightly packed as a metaphor in a poem, and when we read these words, a nuclear core of understanding deepens within us.

Close to the end of a chapter titled "Psychology and Literature" in *The Spirit in Man, Art, and Literature,* Jung observed that "every creative person is a duality or a synthesis of contradictory qualities. On the one side he is a human being with a personal life, while on the other he is an impersonal creative process.... But he can be

---

16 Jung, *CW15,* ¶ 152.
17 Slattery, *Twisted Sky: Selected Poems,* 28.

understood as an artist only in terms of his creative achievement."[18] Anchoring the creative side of my life in fertile ground so it can bear fruit is what Jung's writing has allowed me to do. I would never have thought that a psychologist could become one of the most poignant and often mythopoetic writers on the human imagination, but this is exactly what Jung did, and for some forty years I have turned to his writing for inspiration and guidance.

My hope is that readers who come to this collection of essays will not turn Jung into a deity but will rather see him as someone with whom they can engage in conversation. The time that you invest in his writings will expand the orbit of your own awareness and put you in closer intimacy with your own personal myth.

References

Jung, C.G.. *Modern Man in Search of a Soul.* New York: Harcourt, Brace, 1933.

————. "The Spirit in Man, Art and Literature." *The Collected Works of C. G. Jung, Vol. 15.* Translated by R.F.C. Hull. New York: Pantheon Books, 1966.

May, Rollo. *Love and Will.* New York: Norton, 1969.

Melville, Herman. *Moby Dick.* New York: Norton, 1967.

Slattery, Dennis Patrick. *Casting the Shadows: Selected Poems.* Kearney, New Hampshire: Morris Publishing Co, 2001.

————. *Just Below the Water Line: Selected Poems.* Goleta, California: Winchester Canyon Press, 2004.

————. *Twisted Sky: Selected Poems.* Goleta, California: Winchester Canyon Press, 2007.

Slattery, Dennis Patrick, and Chris Paris. *The Beauty Between Words: Selected Poems.* Stormville, New York: Water Forest Press, 2010.

---

18 Jung, *CW15,* ¶ 157.

I Only Ever Wanted to be a Bus Driver
An Unfinished Life

by Robert D. Romanyshyn, Ph.D.

The Berlin Zoo/1965

I first met Carl Jung in front of the chimpanzee cages at the Berlin Zoo in the summer of 1965. Of course, he had already died, and so the meeting was a bit peculiar for someone like myself who, at 22, did not have much experience with the dead. Having grown up in a house with few books, I was nevertheless blessed with an Irish mother and a Ukrainian father who, at our Sunday ritual dinner table, opened the world of imagination to me. They were good storytellers, especially my father, and sitting between them I soaked up the richness and beauty of words and their power to create unseen realities. When the stories began on those Sunday after-dinner afternoons, a curtain would rise, and in place of the quotidian world of plates and pot roast, knives and forks, teacups and cakes, a drama would begin.

My two favorite stories, and the ones that had the most magic for me, were the tales my father told of his orphan wanderings in the post World War I landscapes of Eastern Europe, and the one my mother would tell of sitting beside her mother's death bed, thinking her mother had fallen asleep and trying to rouse her to attend to the visitors who had come to the house to mourn her passing. She was four at that time, and that day was a Sunday. In these stories death and mourning, loss and grief, being an orphan, abandonment, and the issue of home were my teachers. These images were the forces that raised the curtain and transformed Brooklyn, New York of the 1950s into those worlds. No camera, of course, could record that change, and yet there it was, as real and present as the dinner on the table.

At the Berlin Zoo, in the summer of 1965, another curtain was raised, and behind it stood Carl Jung. My ticket, as it were, to that drama, which has lasted now almost fifty years, was my copy of *Memories, Dreams, Reflections*.[1] Jung seemed amused, and I think he even chuckled a bit as he noticed the book under my arm. He was avuncular, and I had the distinct feeling that this uncle of the soul had been waiting for me in

---

1 Jung, *Memories, Dreams, Reflections*.

some place beyond time. He was a mood, a quality of the moment, a figure present in his absence, and in that presence I had the sense that my life was enfolded within stories quite outside myself.

I have always suspected we do not chart the course of our lives, but most of my life I resisted that gnawing, insistent suspicion. I had only ever wanted to be a bus driver, content and calm and clear about knowing the way. That was the fantasy I grew up with, the fantasy that suited my world, even as it was always challenged by those Sunday stories. But after the sudden death in 1991 of my wife Janet, to whom I had been married for 25 years, that resistance was shattered,[2] and out of the broken fragments of my life, and in the cauldron of chaos worked in analysis, I realized that I had been a bus driver. Not, of course, the one I had had the fantasy of being, but the one that the image itself had shaped for me. I have not been the one mapping the route and driving the bus, but the one—and I love this phrase because it so fits the experience—who has been taken for a ride by those figures of soul who have been charting the course that has also mapped my life.

We live with the dead and in the ambience of their absent-presence we are not just the authors of our actions but are also agents in service to their unfinished business. As I sit at my desk typing these words, Jung hovers nearby. He still lives. He 'looks' the same as he did nearly fifty years ago, smiling and avuncular but with a sly ironic twist in his smile that turns the question Philemon asked of him—"Do you think you are the thinker of your thoughts?"—back on me: "Do you think you are the driver of the bus?" I do not. The 'monkey business' that began so long ago and quite far away continues.

The Philosopher and the Poet

Several years ago, while finishing a book on an approach to research that would keep soul in mind, and which was strongly influenced by Jung's presence in my study, I found myself re-engaged with the poet Orpheus. The poet has always been in the background of my work with regard to the issue of the language of psychology and the speech of soul. In my first book in 1982, *Psychological Life: From Science to Metaphor*[3] I was guided by the philosopher Maurice Merleau-Ponty's phenomenology of embodi-

---

2 R. Romanyshyn, *The Soul in Grief: Love, Death and Transformation.*
3 R. Romanyshyn, *Psychological Life: From Science to Metaphor.*

ment, within which he showed how language not only arises in the chiasm between the flesh of the body and that of the world, but also how language in all its forms of expression is always a response to the "savage being of the world" (*etre sauvage*), which always leaves as much unsaid as is said.

How close this philosopher seemed to me to the poet Rilke, who in his *Duino Elegies* asked, "Earth, isn't this what you want: an invisible re-arising in us?," a question preceded by an earlier one in which he asked, "Are we, perhaps, here just for saying: House/Bridge, Fountain, Gate, Jug, Olive tree, Window—/possibly: Pillar, Tower? …"[4] Reading those passages, I was always struck by the way in which two simple words—perhaps/possibly—capture that element of uncertainty in our response ability. Poet and philosopher each acknowledging that language begins with listening, that it begins in the ear and not on the tongue, and each in their different, distinctive voices, one philosophical, the other poetic, being responsible to what calls them into speaking.

As much types as specific figures of soul whose subtle presence is neither a matter of fact nor an idea of mind, these two held for me that question of how does one say and write down the soul. At times, my study became very crowded with other members of these two tribes.

Was I as a psychologist, a philosopher, or a poet? How does one choose between two positions? Although I had met Jung in 1965, he was and had been a rather quiet passenger between that year and 1982, and I had neither knowledge of, nor, if I had, the patience to practice active imagination as a way of waiting in the space of the tension of opposites. I was young and willful and still quite psychologically deaf.

Torn between the philosopher and the poet, I frequently sided with the rigor and shining clarity of the philosopher's speech, and doing so banished the poet from the study. But occasionally I was seduced by the beauty and elusive ambiguity of the poet's voice. Although I could sense that I was a different person when I was reading or thinking or writing in the company of the philosophers from what and who I was when in the company of the poets, I still struggled in those moments when the curtain between these two worlds would open and the landscape of the study would change.

---

4 Rilke, *Duino Elegies.*

The mood of the study was always more melancholic when the poet was present and the atmosphere more soft and dreamlike, the things of the room drifting beyond their sharp corners and edges as if each thing in some kind of rush of erotic longing was bleeding itself out toward other things.

But against the hardness of the desk and the chairs, these shifts in the landscapes that felt so real were a mere poetic fantasy.

In this ambience, I remained reasonable and resolved the tension between these two modes of saying soul on the side of the philosopher. The result, which I did not intend or foresee, was a book whose philosophical argument about the metaphorical character of psychological life was rigorously clear about the poetic ambiguity of metaphor. And yet the poet, not so obedient to my will, lingered in the margins and between the lines. And in this place of ambiguous clarity, Jung was waiting. Some unfinished business still lurked in the question about the language of psychology and the speech of soul.

The Metaphoric Image and the Imaginal Life of Soul

Seventeen years earlier I had met Carl Jung in the Berlin Zoo, and now, in 1982, I had finished a book whose ironic consequence was undeniable. Making the argument for metaphor, I had shown that a metaphor both says what something *is not* even as it says what it *is*. But to advocate for a way of saying and writing down soul that would hold the tension between *is/is not*, that would advocate for a way of saying and writing down the soul that makes meaning by un-making it, runs counter to the mindset of most of psychology. Psychology demands that its language be definitive, as the most recent initiative in the American Psychological Association indicates. This initiative wants to define education in psychology in terms of the acronym STEM—Science, Technology, Engineering, and Mathematics. In that context, if a psychologist's language is to be valid, then the relation between what is said, measured, etc., and what is spoken of or measured has to be fixed and precise. In short, the psychologist has to be bloody literal minded.

A way of saying and writing that moves between coagulating meaning and dissolving it, that holds the tension between *is/is not* is not definitive, and its validity is not a matter of a method that prescribes meaning but of truth that is continuously unfolding in a dialogue between being addressed and being responsive. Jung not only understood this point, he championed it. Recognizing that the reality of the unconscious requires us to acknowledge "our view of the world can be but a provisional one," he gave this fine example of its practice. Referring to his patients who needed some stable point if they were not to get lost in the material, he says that he would qualify his interpretations by "interspersing them with innumerable 'perhaps' and 'ifs' and 'buts'… to let the interpretation … trail off into a question whose answer was left to the free fantasy activity of the patient."[5]

Jung's provisional way of saying and writing down soul acknowledges not only the gap between word and soul but also the paradox and ambiguity that animates that gap. A metaphor *alludes* to what something is and means and leaves it and its meaning *elusive*. In their Latin root—*ludere*—these two terms situate the use of language within an attitude of play. In the context of metaphor the psychologist can no longer take his words, ideas, or facts literally or even seriously. In alluding to the subtle epiphanies of soul that remain forever elusive, slipping the nets woven by mind, the psychologist has to use his or her words, ideas and facts metaphorically and playfully. For the epiphanies of soul, the definitive language of non-contradiction and precision has to give way to a language of paradox and ambiguity.

Jung's provisional way of saying and writing down soul is steeped in a metaphoric sensibility that opens that third space of the image that is neither a thing nor a thought. As such, a metaphoric sensibility is responsive to the unique reality of soul as that third domain of the image, which is grasped neither by the scientific language of empirical facts nor the rational language of logical ideas. Henri Corbin, whose influence on Jung was extensive, described this third domain of soul as an imaginal reality, which mediates between the mind of intellect and the world of the senses.[6] It is a domain of reality where the poet seems more at home than either the scientist or the philosopher.

This was not where I had expected to end up. I thought I had known where I was going. I thought that I was the one who was actively making the map, but it was Jung, along with others, sitting patiently and quietly in the bus and perhaps even smiling, who were charting the course. Moreover, when I finished the book on metaphor, Jung not only did not get off the bus, he moved from the back of it to the front. From 1982 through 2007, and through many detours, especially the descent into grief when my

5 Jung, "On the Nature of the Psyche," *CW8*, ¶¶ 369, 400.
6 Corbin, *Alone with the Alone: Creative Imagination in the Sufism of Ibn' Arabi.*

wife suddenly died and the bus went off the road and fell into the abyss, the unfinished business about language and soul took surprising turns.

The maps charting the route now were Jung's writings on alchemy, the subtle world of the *unus mundus* and the psychoid archetype. While in this span of time I had my hands upon the wheel, I increasingly realized Jung was taking me for a ride. Along this route I have come to appreciate more deeply three ways that Jung has changed my life.

First, I have come to understand and to appreciate the autonomous reality of the psyche and its imaginal figures. This is and continues to be a very humbling and even humiliating experience, an experience that pushes me back into the *humus*, the native ground and soil of soul. In these moments when I feel driven there is a psychological obligation to get in touch with *who* is doing the driving, an obligation to be receptive to the imaginal figures in the psyche *who* are addressing me. To meet this obligation requires that I engage in the process of active imagination, and indeed, that process has become a ritual practice for me. Jung's *Red Book*[7] is a powerful and beautiful example of this process, as is Naomi Lowinsky's *The Sister from Below.*[8]

But the obstacles to becoming receptive in this way are not only personal, they are also collective and cultural. An amusing but at the same time rather dark example is the spellchecker on our computers. When I use the passive voice, which is a way of speaking that questions the privileged position of the ego mind as agent, the programmed spell checker in our computers is a collective, anonymous censor of its use. And so, while I would not choose now to say that along the way I have dreamed of Jung, but that along the way I have been dreamed by Jung, my computer advises me to correct that way of speaking.

Second, I have come to understand and to appreciate that in the company of the dead, in the ambience of the ancestors, we are summoned to take up some unfinished business, and that in doing so we are offered our freedom to transform fate into a heritage that becomes a destiny.

Third, I have come to understand and to appreciate that while the work that is taken up is done, it is never finished. This business about language and soul that began in the presence of the "monkey mind" goes on.

---

7 Jung, *The Red Book.*
8 Lowinsky, *The Sister from Below: When the Muse Gets Her Way.*

Between Thinking and Dreaming

While there are many curtains between many worlds, the curtain between thinking and dreaming is perhaps the most fixed. If depth psychology began with the dream as the royal road to the unconscious, that road has been the one less taken, at least since Descartes ran down the curtain between soul and mind and identified the "I" with the thinking mind: *Cogito ergo Sum*.

In 2007, my book, *The Wounded Researcher: Research with Soul in Mind,*[9] was published. An application of the issue of language and soul to the process of research, the book parts the curtain between thinking and dreaming, between a researcher's conscious claims about the work and his or her unconscious ties to the work. Offering numerous examples of how a researcher is claimed by a work through his or her complex wounds as much as he or she chooses it, it lays out processes and methods, which, in making a place for dreams, intuitions, feelings, synchronicities and other expressions of the unconscious, transform a wound into a work. Perhaps, however, the clearest example is the book itself, which was born in between the dreaming soul and thinking mind. Two of those dreams show how psyche kept working the issue of the philosopher and the poet, working like an alchemist in the dark light of soul, continuously dissolving ideas that had become fixed and then coagulating new ones. These two dreams are presented here. Two other dreams are described in the last two chapters of the book, and powerfully illustrate that even as I thought I was done with the book it was not finished dreaming itself through me.

The first dream occurred at the start of the fifth attempt to write the book. The landscape of the dream was my study. In order to appreciate how the circumstances of ordinary life are transformed in the wonderful alchemy of the dream's wisdom, I need to describe the study at that moment in my life.

Two desks were in my study. On one desk was the manuscript for the book on research, which in life had stalled around questions about who was writing the book, for whom was it being written, and why after numerous false starts had the work finally begun in a reverie in a garden in Governor's Bay, outside Christchurch, New Zealand. The introduction that came out of that reverie turned out to be the beginning that would bring the project to its completion, and when I had written it I knew I had sided with the poet more openly and directly than ever before in my work. "Towards

---

9 R. Romanyshyn, *The Wounded Researcher: Research with Soul in Mind*.

a Poetics of the Research Process" was a confession that what mattered in this work was the open admission of "the difference between the fullness of experience and the failure of language to say it, and the sweetly bitter sense of this knowledge."[10]

Over the course of some eighteen months the book would be written and completed in the gap between soul and the words we use to say it, and in that gap it would be the poets who would guide the way. The poetic voice that had earlier been exiled in my writing was now front and present. In the company of Eliot and Keats, of Wallace Stevens and Rainer Maria Rilke, Orpheus came singing into the work, bending it toward a way of saying that would forget psychology for the sake of being psychological, attuning the ear to the sweet and seductive rhythms of language and the hidden roots of words, where, for example, research could be heard as re-search, as a searching again for what had already made its claim upon a researcher, indicating that research as re-search was a vocation, a being called into a work and its unfinished business.

But did I have such courage to declare so openly, to shout as it were in the halls of academia, that psychology requires a poetics of the soul? Could I stand by my confession that, as a psychologist, I was and had always been a "failed poet"? and that being a failed poet for the sake of tending soul was better than being a successful psychologist whose deadly seriousness expressed in calculated language and loveless speech could make one seriously dead?

The other desk in my study at that time had a manuscript I was preparing for a special edition of a journal devoted to Orpheus. It seemed a propitious moment since Orpheus, who had haunted my writing over the years, was now so central to the book on research. But the two projects situated on two different desks vied each morning for my attention.

I loved the research and writing I was doing for the Orpheus project, and I was frustrated with what felt like a lapse in courage to continue the poetics of the research process. I was stretched between the poet figure of Orpheus, who seemed to be beckoning me from some point ahead of me, and my academic self, who seemed to be pulling me back into a familiar and comfortable form. Had I not learned anything from the earlier struggles? Had I learned it but still was not translating what I knew into practice? The old tension of opposites between the philosopher and the poet seemed to be in full play again, as I sunk deeper into that tension as I began to craft,

10 R. Romanyshyn, *The Wounded Researcher: Research with Soul in Mind*, 5.

quite philosophically, the piece on Orpheus within the context of the Orphic roots in Jung's psychology. No wonder alchemy was always beginning the process of fixing and dissolving its materials.

Then something like a miracle happened when my wife mentioned to me a passage in a letter that Jung had written to Aniela Jaffe in 1954 in response to a novel she had sent to him. The novel had been written by Hermann Broch and was called *Der Todd des Vergil*. Reading the letter, I was stunned by Jung's words. Wondering about his reluctance that had over the years held him back from letting the "death of Vergil" approach him too closely, he confesses, "I was jealous of Broch because he has succeeded in doing what I had forbid myself on pain of death." Continuing, he says he had always heard "a voice whispering to me that I could make it (his psychological work) 'aesthetic.'" But he had refused to do so because he feared, "I would have produced nothing but a heap of shards which could never have been turned into a pot." Then in words that seem to echo some painful realization of what he may have lost, Jung writes, "In spite of this ever present realization the artist homunculus in me has nourished all sorts of resentments and has obviously taken it very badly that I didn't press the poet's wreath on his head." As if to underscore the point, Jung asks in a P.S., in that place outside the margins as it were, "Anyway why did it have to be the death of the poet?"[11]

The Dream of the Two Desks

> *As I enter my study, the two desks so separate in waking life have become one. The Orpheus essay published in 2004 is on top of The Wounded Researcher published in 2007. As I look down on the two books, the words of the research text can be seen through the words of the Orpheus essay. In the dream, I know that the two voices belong together, that they can sing in harmony with and echo each other, that the language of academic scholarship can be filtered through the mouth of the poet.*

The second dream occurred shortly after the book was published.

---

11 Jung, *Letters 1951-1961.*

The Dream of Exiting the House of Academia

I am in an old Victorian style house, in an ornately furnished parlor, filled with heavy furniture and with thick drapes on the windows. The room is dimly lit and has an old, musty smell to it. I see a circle of Jungian academics, and many of them are familiar to me. They are conversing with each other in hushed and serious tones, and all of them are dressed in suits and ties. Enclosed within their circle my presence is unnoticed, and I feel invisible.

I leave the parlor and begin to wander through the house and eventually find myself in a middle room. It is spacious and quite empty of furniture but still rather dimly lit. A man dressed in casual attire approaches me. I notice that he has a rather rough-hewn style. His fingers are tobacco stained and his teeth are neither perfectly straight nor pearly white. In his presence and attire he is a stark contrast to the well suited and tied academics, and he impresses me as someone who has lived a full and exciting life. He lets me know that he is a poet and is on the way to teach a young woman about Rilke. When I see them together there is an obvious erotic charge between them, and I feel jealous because I feel I should be teaching the woman about Rilke.

Feeling alone, I walk through the house again and wind up in the kitchen, where the food is cooked to serve the academics. The kitchen is filled with sunlight, which streams through a screen door. The air is warm, and I can smell the aromas of summer outside the house. Outside there is a park where I can see people having a picnic on the green grass, children playing games, and young lovers strolling hand in hand. The dream ends with the poet and me standing on the threshold as he holds the screen door open to the world.

I have worked with this dream in analysis and in active imagination, and it continues to inspire my life. There are many interpretations of it, and I am sure that many of them are quite obvious to anyone with knowledge of Jungian dream work. But in the context of this article I want to emphasize only two images that continue to stand out for me.

First, the tension of opposites between the philosopher and the poet has been a journey through many rooms. Second, the journey ends with the poet as the guide and teacher of soul and with me standing with him on the threshold between the world's epiphanies and the world of the academy.

An Unfinished Life

I am sitting in my study looking at the tall green ferns outside an open window, watching their graceful dance in the gentle morning breeze, feeling the cool, fresh air of the day on my skin, smelling the fragrances of the garden, knowing that the threshold between the epiphanies of life and the words we use to say it is where I began, and thinking of these words of T.S. Eliot:

> We shall not cease from exploration
> And the end of all our exploring
> Will be to arrive where we started
> And know the place for the first time.[12]

So, have I made any progress? That, it seems to me, is not the question. Progress is a fiction of mind that depends on time stretching itself out as a line. For the soul, time is a spiraling pivot of the now and the eternal in whose vortex we do not make progress; we deepen into the question(s).

From splitting the poet and the philosopher, to understanding the provisional character of psychological language means our words always and only allude to soul, to the dream image where poet and philosopher sing a duet, to the dream image of the threshold, I have been drawn back to where I began and know it as if for the first time.

On the threshold, in the gap, on the edges of psychology where one can give up psychology for the sake of being psychological, I live my life in ritual and regard with slowness and stillness in the company of the ancestors, knowing through the heart they are a living reality, and attending to the dream. I find it therefore not at all sur-

12 Eliot, *Four Quartets.*

prising that this journey, which began in Berlin in 1965, should have taken me to the Antarctic in 2009. That odyssey, which began with a dream in 1975, has deepened the issue of language and the soul. In the awful and terrible beauty of that landscape, I experienced in a bodily way what Jung has described as the psychoid archetype, that level of the unconscious where what we call the unconscious is the consciousness of nature in us.[13] In that polar wilderness, at the southern end of the *Axis Mundi*, psyche and nature are indeed one.

In moments the "I" who I am dissolved into the white expanse of the ice, seduced into a desire for merger with the seductive siren calls of those towering crystal cathedrals. On my return, I knew that I had some obligation to tell this story, but I also knew that I could not begin with words. The question that has haunted my journey with Jung, the question of the gap between soul and words, was lived in that landscape in ways heretofore only I knew. I understood that language is not in us; we are in it. I understood that the word that is made flesh begins not on the tongue but in the ear, and like the Mary of the Annunciation images, we are impregnated by the flesh of the world, inspired to become its spokesperson. And so, I worked with a composer to set eighty-six of the images to music with a voice over whose words came from the landscape.[14]

Returning to the Poet

Jung is not dead! He is a living reality. His psychology is not just a body of work to be known. It is a way of living in the world, a continuous practice that calls one into his or her individuated life. On the road with Jung from Berlin in 1965 to Summerland, California in 2011, I have been trying to live the life I was meant to live. And on this threshold at this moment, I find some courage to embrace the poet I had not had before. So I end this essay with gratitude and humility for what I have been given along the way and with a poem that is now part of a book of poems in progress called *Leaning toward the Poet*.

---

13 Jung, "On the Nature of the Psyche," *CW 8*.
14 R. Romanyshyn, *Antarctica:Inner Journeys in the Outer World*, C.D, 2010.

Sitting with V in the Morning

It always starts the same way
with hot coffee, buttered toast,
and the newspaper, bought every morning,
set out on the table.

I like these few moments of preparation
before V awakens from sleep and joins me in the garden.
I like especially the cloudy mornings,
when the trees and flowers in the garden are still sleepy,
their vibrant green still folded inside the darkness of night,
and even the birds are still at rest.
Sometimes, while hovering over the birds of paradise,
a hummingbird's wings beat more slowly than usual,
as if it has not yet decided to be a hummingbird that day.
Mist that rises from the ocean climbs the Summerland hills,
moving without resistance or weight,
carrying the water's dreams of becoming green.

"I had a dream last night," she says.
The sun brightens, the mist begins to fade away,
the flowers and trees shake off their dark covers,
and the hummingbird beats its wings more frantically.
I wonder at this marvel,
of how the sun brightens with the saying of the words,
of how the trees and flowers shake off their dark cover,
become more green and seem to stand at attention,
curious, perhaps?, to hear the dream,
and of how the hummingbird now flits and darts
among the flowers and trees,

whispering with excitement about what is to come.

But I also wonder if the ocean's misty dreams

are comfortable with their surrender to ours.

Now it is the two of us in the garden.

I turn my gaze away from the flowers,

the trees, and the birds,

put the paper aside, take another sip of coffee and listen.

Making sense of the dream together,

V and I are making love.

But the misty dreams of the ocean

that need no interpretation are gone,

and in this moment I know

that each morning we enact again the story of the fall.

When she leaves,

when the coffee is finished or is now too cold to drink,

I look again at the flowers and trees,

I listen to the birds that are still there,

but now they are all a little farther away.

References

Corbin, Henry. *Alone with the Alone: Creative Imagination in the Sufism of Ibn'Arabi.* Princeton: Princeton University Press, 1997.

Eliot, T.S. *Four Quartets.* New York: Harcourt Brace, 1943/1971.

Jung, C.G. "On the Nature of the Psyche." *The Collected Works of C.G. Jung, Vol. 8.* Translated by R.F.C. Hull. Princeton: Princeton University Press, 1947/1969.

———. *Memories, Dreams, Reflections.* New York: Random House, 1961.

———. *Letters 1951–1961.* Ed. Gerhard Adler. Princeton: Princeton University Press, 1975.

———. *The Red Book.* New York: W.W. Norton and Company, 2009.

Lowinsky, Naomi Ruth. *The Sister From Below: When the Muse Gets Her Way.* Carmel, CA: Fisher King Press, 2009.

Rilke, Ranier Maria. *Duino Elegies.* New York: W.W. Norton and Company, 1939.

Romanyshyn, Robert. *Psychological Life: From Science to Metaphor.* Austin: Texas University Press, 1982. Republished as *Mirror and Metaphor: Images and Stories of Psychological Life.* Pittsburgh: Trivium Publications, 2001.

——— *The Soul in Grief: Love, Death and Transformation.* Berkeley: North Atlantic, 1999.

——— *The Wounded Researcher: Research with Soul in Mind.* New Orleans: Spring Journal Books, 2007.

———*Antarctica: Inner Journeys in the Outer World.* DVD and lecture available at www.jungplatform.com.

Drunk with Fire

by Naomi Ruth Lowinsky

How *The Red Book* Transformed My Jung

Support me for I stagger, drunk with fire. I climbed down through the centuries and plunged into the sun far at the bottom. And I rose up drunk from the sun...

—*The Red Book* [1]

A Distant Fire

There has been a breach between C.G. Jung and me. How could that happen? I had no idea who I was until I met Jung, nor had I had a decent conversation with my soul. Jungian analysis showed me my way into the world, and into my inner life—it opened the door to the poet I'd left behind in my childhood. But when I encountered Jung's suspicious attitude toward artists—so like a Swiss burgher—the poet in me was offended.

Enter *The Red Book*. When I sat down with that enormous tome on my lap and leafed through its gloriously illuminated pages, its visionary poetry, its astounding paintings and mandalas, my heart opened to my illustrious ancestor—all was forgiven. I felt vindicated. Jung, as I'd always suspected, was a closeted poet.

What is this *Red Book*? During a difficult time in his life, after his break with Freud, Jung was deluged with powerful images and visions. He wrote them down and painted them. He created a strange and beautiful book—bound in red leather—to hold them. It looks like a medieval illuminated manuscript. *The Red Book* was not published, even after his death, because of concerns that its wild, prophetic tone would cause people to dismiss Jung as a mystic or a madman. When it finally came out in 2009, it surprised the Jungian world by

---

1 Jung, *The Red Book,* 272.

151

creating a media sensation and selling out its first printing. But, I am getting ahead of my story. Before I tell you how Jung and I reconciled, how we became drinking buddies by the primordial fire, let me give you some history of our relationship.

I first met Jung in my late twenties, when I found *Man and His Symbols* on a remainder table. I didn't know what I was buying into. There he was, in the frontispiece photo, the wise professor at his desk with his pipe and his books—mysterious images glowing behind him. Jung's essay "Approaching the Unconscious" was introduced by an unforgettable photo: doorways within doorways grew smaller and darker, pulling the eye from the opening door frame decorated with Egyptian figures deep into the unknown of the tomb of Ramses III.

At the time I was lost in my life, a single mother of three, full of terrors and complexes, with no sense of self. In a Jungian analysis I felt seen and heard for the first time in my life. I learned to listen to the unconscious, to the charged magnetism of dreams, and to heed the rich vein of inspiration that arises mysteriously from within to guide a life. My Jungian path was revealed; my fire was lit. Jung has been a teacher, a wise man, a guide to a deeply lived life, ever since. But my experience of Jung's fire has been hermetic—from an unseen place in the center of the earth.

Years ago, when I began consulting with Joseph Henderson—one of the founders of the San Francisco Institute who had been in analysis with Jung—I dreamt that in the middle of Joe's consulting room there was a round stove, which Joe called a "funda." I knew that its heat came from the center of the earth. *Funda*—foundational, at the bottom, at the base. *Funda—fundus*—a word for womb. Heat from the womb of the earth is a good image for the fire from the depths that my Jungian training tended. But it was a distant, impersonal fire. And Jung was a distant figure, sitting at his desk full of alchemical and magical texts.

He showed up in a dream as a trickster, waggling his eyebrows like Groucho Marx, handing Joseph Henderson some pieces of silver to hand on to me. It wasn't Jung himself, but his wife Emma, who, in a dream, helped me dress for an upcoming meeting with the Certifying Committee in which I hoped to become a Jungian analyst. She gave me a blouse embroidered with a large tree of life. It looked like the oak tree I'd known as a girl. That oak had given me her lap to sit in: she had given me her strength, her calm, her roots, her far-reaching green hands. In her embrace I'd daydream and write poetry. With the help of Emma Jung and that oak, I was certified.

Despite his distance, Jung and his followers—my analysts, consultants, teachers, colleagues—gave me the tools I needed to follow my own charged path. I found my way back to that oak, and to the poet I'd been as a girl. This is when Jung and I began having problems. Now that I was both an analyst and a poet I was upset by his distrust of artists. There is a passage in *Memories, Dreams, Reflections* in which Jung expresses this distrust. He is writing down his "fantasies"—that is, working on *The Red Book*—and asks himself:

> "What am I really doing? Certainly this has nothing to do with science. But then what is it?" Whereupon a voice within me said, "it is art." I was astonished. It had never entered my head that what I was writing had any connection with art. Then I thought, "Perhaps my unconscious is forming a personality that is not me, but which is insisting on coming through to expression."[2]

Having understood that he had an inner figure whom he called the *anima*, Jung went on to accuse her, and artists, of treachery, even of psychopathology:

> What the anima said seemed to me full of a deep cunning. If I had taken these fantasies of the unconscious as art, they would have carried no more conviction than visual perceptions, as if I were watching a movie. I would have felt no moral obligation toward them. The anima might then have easily seduced me into believing that I was a misunderstood artist, and that my so-called artistic nature gave me the right to neglect reality.[3]

Neglect reality? No moral obligation? Was Jung buying into that tired old stereotype of the artist as a big child, an *enfant terrible*? The artists I know use their creative work to attend to what's real and what's ethical—that's how they get below the surface to touch the essence of things. Poetry and prose are how I express my moral obligation to the dead, to the suffering, to the neglected in myself and in the world.

In most of his writings, Jung keeps a studied distance from the direct experience of the charged path, from the pandemonium of the irrational. If he's drunk with fire, he's holding his liquor well. Though I can understand, rationally, why Jung would need to be a "suit" rather than a "creative," a scientist rather than a poet—why he would need to look relatively sober in his *Collected Works*—I have felt wounded by his dismissive attitude toward the artist, hurt that this powerful ancestor misunderstood the very development in me that his psychology had helped me claim. There was a breach between Jung and me—we tended different fires, honored different lineages, though I never tired of

2 Jung, *Memories, Dreams, Reflections*, 185.
3 Jung, *Memories, Dreams, Reflections*, 187.

pointing out to my inner Jung, in teaching and in writing, that his ancestor and mine—Goethe—was a poet.

Soul's Fire

With the publication of *The Red Book*, my Jung has been transformed. He is "outed" as a poet and a painter. He writes directly out of his vulnerability, working out his relationship with his soul in the depths of the mythopoetic imagination, just as I do. In *The Red Book* Jung reclaims his soul—or rather she reclaims him. She appears to him and becomes his guide. She is an inner figure with a mind of her own. This honoring of the voice from within, which Jung would later call *active imagination*, is one of his greatest gifts to me. Instead of ignoring or dismissing voices that speak to me from within, Jung taught me to listen and to engage in dialogue with them. When "The Sister from Below"[4] began speaking to me, telling me she was my muse, my soul, my writing life took off.

Recently I dreamt that Gilda Frantz and I were driving north to see Jung. I told her I was excited to see him again, since I had known him as a child. *The Red Book* speaks to the child in me. I grew up in a German-speaking household. Though nowadays my German is rusty and childlike, the sound and feel of the language tugs at a primal place. I feel a resonance with the book's beginning phrase: "*Der Weg des Kommenden*"—the way of what is to come. This is the magnetic pull of what wants to be realized, what yearns to be born. It was the creative task of *The Red Book*—to open Jung to his depths, to redeem his soul and his gods.

Jung's elegant calligraphy and illuminations invoke another aspect of my childhood. My father was a musicologist, a historian of the early Renaissance. His soul spoke to him in illuminated manuscripts. I was drawn to them as well. But I was a first-generation kid trying to look American. None of my friends knew an illuminated manuscript from a comic book. When I was first writing poetry in my twenties, I actually had the idea of illuminating my poems. It was one of those passionate ideas that devoured me. I took a calligraphy class. I made an illuminated version of a poem as a gift to my mother in Chicago. I asked a friend who was traveling there to carry it to her. He left it on the plane—it disappeared into some black hole—as did my plans for further illuminations. It is mysterious and moving to me that Jung did this thing I had longed to do.

---

4 Lowinsky, *The Sister from Below: When the Muse Gets Her Way.*

When he implores, "Support me for I stagger drunk with fire," I feel a tug and am deeply moved. Why is this? They are wildly poetic words—in the Dionysian mode. They take me down to that primal level of religious feeling—worship of the sun, our source. I know the states he describes. To be drunk with fire tells it all—the creative ecstasy—at once wildly enlivening and demonic—fire as Dionysus, fire as Shiva, fire as Pele. Certainly being a poet can mean being drunk with the sun from the bottom of time. One finds oneself climbing "down through the centuries"[5] pursuing a word, an image, a phrase of goat song.

It has been essential for me to write directly out of the experience of being in other realities, rather than describing such states from a safe distance. In *The Red Book*, Jung contains his intense and overwhelming experiences by writing them down, by painting them. I recognize that urge. I have shelves and shelves of journals in which I've worked to contain my own fire, to follow inner figures, to work with poems and with dreams, to dive below the surface of the times to what is moving in the depths. And I always feel better, more grounded, more real to myself after I do.

Primordial Fire

Enter, the Sister from Below. She's got an idea:

Why don't you take your own advice? Do an active imagination with Jung, now that you feel this warm glow of kinship libido for him? Imagine you two are sitting by the primordial fire, as he puts it:

An old secret fire burns between us. The words uttered at the fire are ambiguous and deep and show life the right way.

[We] will respect the holy fire again, as well as the shades sitting at the hearth, and the words that encircle the flames.[6]

This makes me nervous. Jung is the master of active imagination. Is it hubris to invoke him?

But I have learned to listen to the Sister. So I sit down, with my notebook. Jung, I discover, is reluctant. He is not at all sure he wants to engage in this exercise.

Why not? I ask.

---

5 Jung, *The Red Book*, 272.
6 Jung, *The Red Book*, 280.

Because I am a fantasy of yours.

I know that. That's why I referred to "my Jung" in my subtitle. You're like Izdubar, in your own *Red Book* story—the god from the East you can save from Western rationality only by calling him a fantasy. You carry him around in your pocket, like an egg.

Yes, but he embodied Eastern wisdom and philosophy. I was a mere mortal, a man of my own time, far from your fantasy Jung.

I understand that. But you are an ancestor. "Take pains to waken the dead."[7] Those are your words. I don't want you to be dead in me. Just as I've had long conversations and written many poems about my personal dead, and the collective dead, I think it is important for me to have a living relationship with you.

Jung, still looking like Groucho Marx, still hanging on to his trickster nature, waggles his eyebrows at me and says:

OK. I'll talk to you, as long as you never forget I'm a fantasy. What are we going to talk about?

How about poetry and art? How my poetry is the way soul speaks to me, helps me contain what might otherwise burn me up. I think the poetic nature of your writing in *The Red Book* enables you to contain immensities, unbearable intensities.

Well, you need to understand it's never been about art for me. Writing, painting, making The Red Book *was all about trying to grasp the unfathomable, the divine.*

Poetry is that for me, too. I too reach for the unfathomable in words. I do see, however, that there is a difference between your practice and mine. What you made is, I think, very beautiful. But I gather that beauty was not your objective. It is mine. For me it is a form of spiritual devotion to revise and revise. Not so much with my head, but with my body, all my senses. I love what you say about words as symbol:

> The symbol is the word . . . that rises out of the depths of the self as a word of power and great need and places itself unexpectedly on the tongue. . . . If one accepts the symbol, it is as if a door opens leading into a new room whose existence one previously did not know.[8]

---

7 Jung, *The Red Book*, 244.
8 Jung, *The Red Book*, 311.

This describes my experience of feeling my way for just the right word/symbol when working on a poem. It must carry that depth charge that opens new rooms. Here's a poem for you. It has fire in it, and a dream.

i asked for a dream

and because you coughed in the night
i remembered
the fire
painted by the woman
who had been through it all—

        her testimony to the ones who burned—

she mixed her own
colors
red with just the right yellow
    for the blaze

        green with a touch of purple
        for foliage
        violet for the pretty horses
            our flesh sacrifice   O
            the leaping flames to god

you turned in bed and groaned about what
      you wouldn't remember—

the woman who painted fire in my dream
      held it up for me
        to see through[9]

My phrase, "her testimony to the ones who burned," refers to what happened to my people in the Shoah; it refers to my dead, to whom I feel a deep obligation. Like you,

---

9 Lowinsky, *crimes of the dreamer*, 3.

I'm haunted, and I feel a kinship with you, sitting by the primal fire, when I read your words:

> But the spirits of those who die before their time will live, for the sake of our present incompleteness, in dark hordes in the rafters of our houses and besiege our ears with urgent laments, until we grant them redemption …[10]

The Jung of my fantasy responds:

The woman who paints fire in your dream, paints it so you can see through it, not be devoured by it. It's easy to be devoured by the dead.

I know that. I was being devoured until I stumbled into my first Jungian analysis and learned to listen to my dreams. But as you say, one can be "held fast by the dead," they can keep one from one's work, because they demand atonement. Much of my writing is in the service of that atonement. Here's a poem for the dead:

Adagio and Lamentation

when my father's fierce fingers made Bach flow
our dead came in and sat with us a ghostly visitation
and my grandmother sang lieder of long ago

this is how prayer was said in my childhood solo
piano arguing with god adagio and lamentation
when my father's fierce fingers made Bach flow

music accompanied us into the valley of the shadow and lo
Bach was torah Mozart was our rod Schubert led us into contemplation
my grandmother sang lieder remembering long ago

my child's soul was full of glimmerings the glamour of the gone the glow
of candles borne by children into the dark German woods the illumination
Of the evergreen all this I saw and more when my father's fierce fingers

made Bach flow

---

10 Jung, *The Red Book*, 297.

my mother's dead sister my grandfather in a cattle car woe

permeated shadows stirred curtains took up habitation

in my grandmother's body filled every song she sang with how she longed

for long ago

long gone now my grandmother my father although

sometimes I call them back by villanelle by incantation

come my fierce father play for me water my soul in Bach's flow

sing my sad grandmother your song is my covenant with long ago[11]

I see, says Jung, *your family used music as a religious practice, to help them bear the unbearable.*

Yes. Music was the religion of my childhood.

And is your primary motivation for writing to atone to the dead?

I think it was the catalyst that began my writing life. But it's become a much larger project. For me, as I think for you, writing is a way of digesting experience, bearing the unbearable, confronting demons and shadows and wrestling them into some sort of relatedness. So writing testimony to the ones who burned has freed me for other passions. The goddess is one. In my lifetime, She who was reviled, forgotten, forbidden, has been redeemed, brought back into consciousness. You saw this coming in your enthusiasm about the Assumption of Mary. I've seen the goddess catch fire in the consciousness of my generation. Here's a poem about that:

A Brief History of Mothers and Daughters

We were the daughters of girdled mothers, Jell-O mold mothers, mothers schooled

in the uses of Lipton's Dried Onion Soup, mothers who dusted

every other morning, taught their daughters how

to iron a man's long-sleeved shirt: first the collar

then the shoulder yoke, poking the hot metal nose

between white buttons. We were the hungry daughters

---

11 Lowinsky, *Adagio & Lamentation*, 27.

of mothers long severed

from the moon in their thighs, long severed

from what had called them

when they were seventeen. We promised ourselves

never to be our mothers. . . .

We were the daughters of Moon Tide, of Life Lust, of what insisted

on coming through us. We smoked it. We drank it. We ingested its Magic

Mushrooms. We saw molecules dance in a leaf, in a stone. We were daughters

of First People, of rivers, of trees. We belonged

to each other. We belonged to the earth. Mystery

called us by name. . . .

We leapt out of marriages, invoked Forbidden Goddesses—the ones the prophets

railed about—you know who I mean: The Whore

of Babylon, the Golden Serpent, the Temple Dancer. It was She

who moved in our bodies, She who tasted the fruit, She

who was exiled from the Garden—She

whom our mothers never dared

to imagine—sat alone, chanting sultry verses

by the Red Sea. . . .

Everything was possible.

We could leap over the moon

We could chant

      write

            paint

                  dance

                          make love like warm rain

                              make love like wild surf

It was Our Period.[12]

---

12 First published in *The Spoon River Poetry Review*.

You were certainly drunk with that fire! Jung is laughing at me.

Oh, I was. That fire is quieter now, but still illuminates my worlds.

We sit for a while, in silence, watching the primordial fire, my fantasy Jung and I.

Catastrophic Fires

There is a sudden commotion in the air, a rustling of skirts and shawls, and here she is, my Sister from Below, come from the bottom of beyond to join us at the primordial fire.

You might have invited me, she says. *This is my kind of fire.*

You don't usually require an invitation, I say. You just show up. Why now?

I'm here to ask your man Jung a question on your behalf.

Jung looks interested. *Are you this woman's soul?*

I am. But I want to ask you about your soul—her terrible prophesy of fire—not the fire of ecstasy, not the fire of the hearth or this holy fire we sit around—but the fire of catastrophe. Your soul spoke to you and said:

> I see the surface of the earth and smoke sweeps over it—a sea of fire rolls in from the north, it is setting the towns and villages on fire, plunging over the mountains, breaking through the valleys, burning the forests—people are going mad.[13]

The Sister says: *I too see terrible fires. I too prophesy catastrophic times. You were a mortal, how did you tolerate that fire?*

I jump in before Jung can speak: in my life I have lurched from fear of the fire I came from—the Shoah—to fear of fire as atom bomb, as Agent Orange, as suicide bomber, as global warming. There's always something new to fear. How did you stand it?

Jung sighs. *With great difficulty. The fire threatened to engulf me. It took painting mandalas. It took major efforts on the part of my soul Izdubar, Philemon, and all the others. My soul told me I had to sacrifice fear—a difficult thing to do. One has to keep sacrificing it everyday, sometimes with every breath, like meditation, like yoga.*

You listened to your soul, to your muse, says the Sister from Below, *and made a work of art to hold yourself together. Your soul knew that writing and painting are magic.*

---

13 Jung, *The Red Book*, 346.

I join in. Poems are magic. They are prayers, invocations, spells. I love what you say about magic:

> Everything that works magically is incomprehensible, and the incomprehensible often works magically. The magical opens spaces that have no doors and leads one out into the open where there is no exit. We need magic to be able to receive or invoke the messenger and the communication of the incomprehensible. Magic is a way of living. If one has done one's best to steer the chariot, and one then notices that a greater other is actually steering it, then magical operation takes place.[14]

My Jung is laughing at me again. *I can see what you're up to. You're trying to convince me that I'm an artist after all, because* The Red Book *saved me, as your writing saves you. But it saved me to become who I was—not an artist but an empirical scientist of soul. I stopped using words like* magic *so people would take me seriously. But you and I can agree that magic exists, that it is a way of living, of working, that it inhabits language.*

My Sister from Below speaks to me now: *You don't need Jung to call himself an artist. You just need to remember that his soul and I are sisters from the bottom of time. You know from me, you know from him that you need to surrender in order to feel a "greater other" steering your work, taking you some place you didn't know you needed to go. When you started this paper, you didn't know you'd be sitting by the holy fire with your fantasy Jung and me, now did you? Thanks to me, thanks to him, you've "squandered"[15] decades on this opus of wandering inner worlds, writing poems that steer you into a new way of seeing. Jung has said: "This life is the way, the long sought after way to the unfathomable which we call divine."[16] Poems are your way. I think of your poem "Psalm"; like the psalmist of old, you are struggling to find meaning amidst the catastrophic fires of your times. End with it. Your readers may need it.*

---

14 Jung, *The Red Book*, 314.
15 Jung, *The Red Book*, 330.
16 Jung, *The Red Book*, 232

Psalm

descend upon me   you who are source

before source   fire in the sky   gleam

in the back of my skull   come in the wind

with wings   come in my breath   i cling

to the luminous stair   sing me your names—

spirit   void   darkening sea   world

tree—when thunder speaks   come into my heart

where terrible stories are told—

                the woman

whose womb has cast pieces of flesh   all over the streets

of Jerusalem   that son of your prophet   whose light

splintered   into thousands of dangerous

shards—   i gather it all for the altar

      the blood   the rage   the weeping

             show me your face

                in the fire[17]

---

17 First published in Lowinsky, "Wrestling with God: From the Book of Job to the Poets of the Shoah."

References

Jung, C.G. *Memories, Dreams, Reflections.* New York: Vintage Books, 1965.

———. *The Red Book.* New York: W. W. Norton and Company, 2009.

Lowinsky, N. R. *Adagio & Lamentation.* Carmel, CA: Fisher King Press, 2010.

———. *crimes of the dreamer.* Oakland, CA: Scarlet Tanager Books.

———. *The Sister from Below: When the Muse Gets Her Way.* Carmel, CA: Fisher King Press, 2009.

———. "Wrestling with God: From the Book of Job to the Poets of the Shoah." In *Terror, Violence, and the Impulse to Destroy.* John Beebe, Ed. Switzerland: Daimon Verlag, 2003.

Glossary

Active imagination: The practice of connecting to inner figures or relating to inner realities through the arts.

Alchemy: Ancient practice dedicated to the transformation of matter and spirit.

Analysand: The patient of a Jungian analyst.

Archetype: Patterns or motifs that recur in myth, religion, dreams—and the human psyche. Example: the Trickster.

Anima/Animus: Contrasexual figure in one's psyche.

Calcinatio: Alchemical process of burning the dross, used to describe a psychological state.

Coagulatio: Alchemical process of coagulating, used to describe a psychological state.

Collective unconscious: Archetypes, memories and other material shared by all humanity across cultures.

Complex: Intense feeling-toned pattern with an archetypal core and connected to personal history, e.g., mother complex.

Daimon/daemon: the spirit of place or person.

Feminine Principle: Receptive (yin) energy.

Hermetic: Secret knowledge as in alchemical or other esoteric practices; insulated from outside influences.

Individuation: The long road to becoming oneself.

Kinship libido: Feeling related through a sense of emotional or cultural resonance.

Masculine principle: Phallic (yang) energy.

Nigredo: Alchemical process of descent into darkness, used to describe a psychological state.

Persona: How we present ourselves to the outer world.

Prima materia: In alchemy the most primal, unworked matter, the subject of the transformation.

Projection: Psychological content projected outward onto others rather than acknowledging that this is one's own material.

Self: Central organizing principle of the psyche, mostly unconscious.

Shadow: the parts of ourselves that we are unconscious of or reject.

Synchronicity: Meaningful coincidence.

Transcendent function: Where unconscious and conscious meet and creativity begins.

Transference/Countertransference: What the analysand projects onto analyst/what the analyst projects onto analysand.

Typology: Jung's system for understanding peoples' orientation to reality. He posits four functions: thinking, feeling, sensation, and intuitive.

Solutio: Alchemical process of dissolving, used to describe a psychological state in Jungian psychology.

Unus mundus: One world. The interpenetration of all things.

Biographical Statements

Henry Abramovitch is training analyst and founding president of Israel Institute of Jungian Psychology. He has served on ethics and program committees of the IAAP and provides supervision to a Developing Group in Poland. He is a professor at Tel Aviv University Medical School and served as president of Israel Anthropological Association and as co-facilitator of Interfaith Encounter Group. He is author of *The First Father* (2nd edition, 2010) and forthcoming volume on brothers and sisters. His special joys are poetry, dream groups, and the holy city of Jerusalem, where he lives with wife and family.

Jerome S. Bernstein, M.A.P.C., NCPsyA., is a Jungian analyst in private practice in Santa Fe, New Mexico. He is a senior analyst on the teaching faculty of the C.G. Jung Institute of Santa Fe of which he is a former president. He was the founding president of the Jungian Analysts of Washington (D.C.). He is the author of *Power and Politics, the Psychology of Soviet-American Partnership* (Shambhala 1989), *Living in the Borderland: The Evolution of Consciousness and the Challenge of Healing Trauma* (Routledge 2005) and is co-editor, along with Philip Deloria, of the groundbreaking book, *C.G. Jung and the Sioux Traditions* by Vine Deloria, Jr. (Spring Books: 2009), in addition to numerous articles concerning international conflict, shadow dynamics in the collective psyche as well as various clinical topics and lectures internationally on these and other subjects.

Patricia Damery is an analyst member of the C.G. Jung Institute of San Francisco in private practice in Napa, California, where she and her husband farm a Biodynamic organic ranch. She has published numerous articles, as well as a book detailing her analytic training and simultaneous entry into Biodynamic farming: *Farming Soul: A Tale of Initiation*. Her novel, *Snakes*, the story about the demise of the family farm and the impact on one family, told through the mythology of the snake, was published by Fisher King Press in March 2011. Her forth coming novel *Goatsong*, a story of the resilience of love, is to be published 2012.

Claire Douglas is a clinical psychologist and Jungian analyst. She trained at the New York Association for Analytical Psychology and has been a training and supervisory analyst with the C.G. Jung Institute of Los Angeles since 1992. She lectures and writes books and articles on Jung and on women's psychology. Her latest, *The Old Woman's Daughter,* was the fourteenth of the Fay Lecture Series. She is deeply grateful to live and still practice in a house on a bluff looking out over the Pacific Ocean.

Gilda Frantz is a writer and Jungian analyst practicing in Santa Monica, California. She is co-editor in chief of *Psychological Perspectives*, a Jungian Journal of World Thought, and is a director of the Philemon Foundation, Emerita. She served on the board for five years, during the planning and publication of *The Red Book*. Gilda lives with her mixed poodle/terrier, Spike.

Jacqueline Gerson is a Jungian analyst with a private practice in Mexico City, where she works as an analyst, teacher, and supervisor. With a life long passion for dance and movement she first approached dreams as spontaneous choreographies created by the psyche. That discovery led her to the study of analytical psychology and eventually to become an individual member of the IAAP. She lectures on topics related to analytical psychology throughout the world and has been published in *The San Francisco Jung Institute Library Journal*, with Daimon Verlag, Brunner-Routledge, *Spring Journal*, as well as the Mexican Magazine *Epoca*.

Sharon Heath is a Jungian analyst in private practice and a faculty member of the C.G. Jung Institute of Los Angeles. She writes fiction and non-fiction exploring the interplay of science and spirit, politics and pop culture, contemplation and community. She has given talks in the United States and Canada on topics ranging from the place of soul in social media to gossip, envy, secrecy, and belonging. She served as associate editor of *Psychological Perspectives* and guest editor of the special issue *The Child Within/The Child Without*. Her novel *The History of My Body* was published by Genoa House in 2011.

Jean Kirsch is a psychiatrist and Jungian analyst practicing in Palo Alto, California. She is married to the Jungian analyst Tom Kirsch, the son of Hilde and James Kirsch, who were instrumental in founding the C.G. Jung Institute of Los Angeles. She is past president of the C.G. Jung Institute of San Francisco, where she continues teaching as a member of the faculty. Her current interests include grandmothering, writing, and teaching analytical psychology, both in San Francisco and for the several developing Jungian groups in Taiwan and mainland China.

Chie Lee is a Jungian analyst with a private practice in Beverly Hills and West Los Angeles. She received a Master's degree in counseling psychology in 1990 from Pacifica Graduate Institute. She was trained at the C.G. Jung Institute of Los Angeles and received her diploma in 2000. Chie has been an active member of the Los Angeles Jungian community. She teaches and supervises in the Institute Training program and serves on the Board and many Committees. She has given seminars on Chinese fairy tale, movie and Avant-Garde art. Chie served as the president of the L.A. Institute from 2010–2012.

Naomi Ruth Lowinsky is an analyst member of the San Francisco C.G. Jung Institute, and a widely published poet. Her recent memoir, *The Sister from Below: When the Muse Gets Her Way* tells stories of her pushy muse. She is also the author of *The Motherline: Every Woman's Journey to Find her Female Roots* and three books of poetry. The most recent is *Adagio & Lamentation*. Lowinsky has written many essays in what she considers her "Jungian memoir" mode. They have been published in *Psychological Perspectives* and in the *Jung Journal*. She teaches and lectures in many settings. She is the winner of the Obama Millennium Award for a poem about Obama's grandmother.

Robert D. Romanyshyn, Ph.D. is a senior core faculty member of the Clinical Psychology Program at Pacifica Graduate Institute and an affiliate member of the Inter-Regional Society of Jungian Analysts. Author of six books, numerous chapters in edited volumes and journal articles, he is currently working on a series of small books that explores outside the boundaries of academia various ways of *saying* soul. Two works in this series are his recently completed DVD, *Antarctica: Inner Journey in the Outer World*, which explores the chiasm among images, music and words, and a book of poems, *Leaning Toward the Poet*.

Dennis Patrick Slattery, Ph.D. is core faculty in the Mythological Studies Program at Pacifica Graduate Institute. He is the author, co-author, editor or co-editor of 17 books, including four volumes of poetry. The author of dozens of articles in journals, magazines and newspapers, Dr. Slattery continues to work in the cross-currents of poetry, myth and depth psychology. He offers Riting Retreats on one's personal myth across the United States and in Europe. His new book, *Day-to-Day Dante: Exploring One's Personal Myth Through The Divine Comedy*, is available on his website. His most recent publication, *Riting Myth, Mythic Writing: Plotting Your Personal Story*, has just been published by Fisher King Press.

Karlyn M. Ward, Ph.D., LCSW, is an analyst member of The C.G. Jung Institute of San Francisco, and is in private practice in Mill Valley, California. She writes and teaches on the relationship of music to the psyche, works with music as an entré to active imagination, and is a Fellow in the Association of Music and Imagery. Her DVD, *Anchored in the Heart: Redeeming the Dark Feminine* explores the implications of the figure of Mary of Magdala in word, art, and music. Her book *Visitation in a Zen Garden* almost wrote itself after a family of grey foxes (parents and four kits) took up residence in the backyard zen garden designed by her husband, Richard Ward. She is continuing to write about her archetypal experiences.

Barbara McCauley lives in Truchas, a mountain village in northern New Mexico where she and husband, Alvaro Cardona-Hine, both write and paint and exhibit their work. Barbara works spontaneously with the paint, and the *Marked By Fire* cover image, "Flight Into Egypt" is one of several paintings of women that simply appeared in the underpainting, and which she then fleshed out. Raised Catholic, she always felt that the depictions of Mary were idealized; when this one appeared, she was delighted to see her as a simple, but strong, woman, Mediterranean in origin, as, if she existed at all, she must certainly have been. Learn more at: www.cardonahinegallery.com

The Fisher King Press Story

A great deal of seduction has been called for to lure me away from the selfish pursuits of fortune, fame, and a vast array of many other vises that I once believed could relieve my existential angst. I must confess that Fisher King Press is the child of one of these many selfish forays.

Several years ago 'by chance' I met a Jungian and began analysis. We worked together for sometime before I gained the courage to leave a well-paying career and the security of an antiquated identity behind. The analysis continued and within a few weeks of leaving this old life, I brought a dream into our session. My analyst suggested a dialogue with one of the dream characters. Little did I know that this would lead to the expansion of my miniature world, the writing of eight novels, and much more.

The writing, like so many other things before, overtook me. I didn't care about publishing a book. I only wanted to write, to create, to selfishly express myself (and my 'self') and for several years I enjoyed the good fortune of just this, living in Europe, frequenting cafes in Italy, France, Switzerland, Ireland . . . encountering characters and weaving tales.

People would ask what I did for a living and my answer would be "I used to be a John Deere tractor salesman." "Yes, but what do you do now?" "Oh, I just live, just enjoy life now." "Yes, but you must do something with your time?" "Well, okay, I write." "A ha, so you are a writer!" "No, I'm not a writer. I just write." "What do you write about?" I'd hesitate and occasionally answer, "I write about dreams. Every morning I get up and write about my dreams, and then I write about life, about how dreams . . . well, about how dreams intersect our lives, our waking lives, how they are tied together . . ."

I sincerely meant what I said, about how dreams intersect our lives and so forth. I believed it and at the same time couldn't completely understand it, as is often still the case. But that was part of the fun, knowing and not-knowing, being in that in-between place, where the mysterious takes holds, where one cannot wrap one's mind around an idea or concept and instead simply must follow the words and images.

So, I continued to follow the words and images when they came in dreams and when they came in waking life. I also continued to explain to others of how I once was a tractor salesman, and then on into the writing thing. Finally one day I grew tired of having to explain about who I once was and how now I wrote, but no, they could not read my writing, and no, I had never published a book . . . So, I sent query letters to a few publishers, expecting to be received with open arms, but quickly learned that I might well spend the rest of my life waiting for someone else to say yes, waiting for someone else to validate me, my existence, who I was becoming, and I said the heck with all that!

Soon after came Fisher King Press and the publication of my first three novels, The Chronicles of a Wandering Soul series: *LeRoi, Menopause Man—Unplugged*, and *SamSara*. Then it was time to find and publish another author, so up went a basic website and not long after came a query from John Atkinson and we contracted to publish *Timekeeper*, Atkinson's novel/quasi-memoir, a coming-of-age tale, describing the experiences of a 14-year-old runaway boy's hardships, victories, and all the inspirational people who guided him on his journey and helped him to triumph over illiteracy. Critics have since praised *Timekeeper* as a deeply moving book written in the spirit of Sue Monk Kidd's *The Secret Life of Bees*.

But what about Jung, how do Jungian publications fit into the Fisher King scheme of things? Well, over the years, I've enjoyed the pleasure of building meaningful and lasting relationships with several Jungian analysts and I also hold a deep respect for the many Jungian publications that have brought understanding to the darker periods of my life. So, it was time to obtain a Centerpoint newsletter and send out a query to the listed Jungian societies and organizations.

April Barrett, executive director of the Jung Society of Washington was quick to forward the request to Lawrence Staples and we soon agreed to publish *Guilt with a Twist: The Promethean Way*. Erel Shalit and *Enemy, Cripple, Beggar: Shadows in the Hero's Path* came next. From there, kind of like following words and images, things began to unfold, and what was originally created from an unconscious inflation to serve my own selfish desires, Fisher King Press finally became what it was meant to be—'Self' Serving.

The Chronicles of a Wandering Soul series is available from Fisher King Press and my other novels will be published as the years unfold, where you'll learn about what an ornery rascal I can be in my endless pursuit to reclaim soul, or should I say, be reclaimed by soul. Sure, there's some goodness in me too, but enough about 'me' and

'I' and all my selfish exploits, and please don't hold this against the other Fisher King Press authors whose worthy publications deserve to be widely read.

We are most grateful to the many readers who purchase Fisher King Press publications and we look forward to bringing you more books as the years unfold. On the next few pages, you will find our current list of publications. You are also invited to visit our website at www.fisherkingpress.com and you may enjoy the many articles posted to our online newsletter at www.fisherkingreview.com.

Mel Mathews,

Publisher, Fisher King Press

Jungian Psychology Titles

Re-Imagining Mary: A Journey Through Art to the Feminine Self
by Mariann Burke, 1ˢᵗ Ed., Trade Paperback, 180pp, Index, Biblio., 2009
— ISBN 978-0-9810344-1-6

Threshold Experiences: The Archetype of Beginnings
by Michael Conforti, 1ˢᵗ Ed., Trade Paperback, 168pp, Index, Biblio., 2008
— ISBN 978-0-944187-99-9

Marked By Fire: Stories of the Jungian Way
edited by Patricia Damery & Naomi Ruth Lowinsky,
1ˢᵗ Ed., Trade Paperback, 180 pp, Index, Biblio., 2012
— ISBN 978-1-926715-68-1

Farming Soul: A Tale of Initiation
by Patricia Damery, 1ˢᵗ Ed., Trade Paperback, 166pp, Index, Biblio., 2010
— ISBN 978-1-926715-01-8

Transforming Body and Soul: Therapeutic Wisdom in the Gospel Healing Stories
by Steven Galipeau, Rev. Ed., Trade Paperback, 180pp, Index, Biblio., 2011
— ISBN 978-1-926715-62-9

Lifting the Veil: Revealing the Other Side
by Fred Gustafson & Jane Kamerling, 1ˢᵗ Ed, Paperback, 170 pp, Biblio, 2012
— ISBN 978-1-926715-75-9

Resurrecting the Unicorn: Masculinity in the 21ˢᵗ Century
by Bud Harris, Rev. Ed., Trade Paperback, 300pp, Index, Biblio., 2009
— ISBN 978-0-9810344-0-9

The Father Quest: Rediscovering an Elemental Force
by Bud Harris, Reprint, Trade Paperback, 180pp, Index, Biblio., 2009
— ISBN 978-0-9810344-9-2

Like Gold Through Fire: The Transforming Power of Suffering
by Massimilla & Bud Harris Reprint, Trade Paperback, 150pp, Index, Biblio., 2009
— ISBN 978-0-9810344-5-4

The Art of Love: The Craft of Relationship
by Massimilla and Bud Harris, 1st Ed. Trade Paperback, 150pp, 2010
— ISBN 978-1-926715-02-5

Divine Madness: Archetypes of Romantic Love
by John R. Haule, Rev. Ed., Trade Paperback, 282pp, Index, Biblio., 2010
— ISBN 978-1-926715-04-9

Eros and the Shattering Gaze: Transcending Narcissism
by Ken Kimmel, 1ˢᵗ Ed., Trade Paperback, 310 pp, Index, Biblio., 2011
— ISBN 978-1-926715-49-0

The Sister From Below: When the Muse Gets Her Way
by Naomi Ruth Lowinsky, 1ˢᵗ Ed., Trade Paperback, 248pp, Index, Biblio., 2009
— ISBN 978-0-9810344-2-3

The Motherline: Every Woman's Journey to find her Female Roots
by Naomi Ruth Lowinsky, Reprint, Trade Paperback, 252pp, Index, Biblio., 2009
— ISBN 978-0-9810344-6-1

The Dairy Farmers Guide to the Universe: Jung and Ecopsychology, Volume 1
by Dennis Merritt 1ˢᵗ Ed., Trade Paperback, 250 pp, Index, Biblio., 2011
— ISBN 978-1-926715-42-1

The Dairy Farmers Guide to the Universe: Jung and Ecopsychology, Volume 2
by Dennis Merritt 1ˢᵗ Ed., Trade Paperback, 250 pp, Index, Biblio., 2012
— ISBN 978-1-926715-43-8

The Dairy Farmers Guide to the Universe: Jung and Ecopsychology, Volume 3
by Dennis Merritt 1ˢᵗ Ed., Trade Paperback, 220 pp, Index, Biblio., 2012
— ISBN 978-1-926715-44-5

The Dairy Farmers Guide to the Universe: Jung and Ecopsychology, Volume 4
by Dennis Merritt 1ˢᵗ Ed., Trade Paperback, 220 pp, Index, Biblio., 2012
— ISBN 978-1-926715-45-2

Becoming: An Introduction to Jung's Concept of Individuation
by Deldon Anne McNeely, 1ˢᵗ Ed., Trade Paperback, 230 pp, Index, Biblio, 2010
— ISBN 978-1-926715-12-4

Animus Aeternus: Exploring the Inner Masculine
by Deldon Anne McNeely, Reprint, Trade Paperback, 196 pp, Index, Biblio, 2011
— ISBN 978-1-926715-37-7

Mercury Rising: Women, Evil, and the Trickster Gods
by Deldon Anne McNeely, Revised, Trade Paperback, 200 pp, Index, Biblio., 2011
— ISBN 978-1-926715-54-4

Four Eternal Women: Toni Wolff Revisited—A Study In Opposites
by Mary Dian Molton & Lucy Anne Sikes1st Ed, 320 pp, Index, Bib, 2011
— ISBN 978-1-926715-31-5

Gathering the Light: A Jungian View of Meditation
by V. Walter Odajnyk, Revised. Ed., Trade Paperback, 264 pp, Index, Biblio, 2011
— ISBN 978-1-926715-55-1

The Promiscuity Papers
by Matjaz Regovec 1st Ed., Trade Paperback, 86 pp, Index, Biblio., 2011
— ISBN 978-1-926715-38-4

Enemy, Cripple, Beggar: Shadows in the Hero's Path
by Erel Shalit, 1st Ed., Trade Paperback, 248pp, Index, Biblio, 2008
— ISBN 978-0-9776076-7-9

The Cycle of Life: Themes and Tales of the Journey
by Erel Shalit, 1st Ed., Trade Paperback, 210pp, Index, Biblio. 2011
— ISBN 978-1-926715-50-6

The Hero and His Shadow: Psychopolitical Aspects of Myth and Reality in Israel
by Erel Shalit, Revised Ed., Trade Paperback, 208pp, Index, Biblio. 2012
— ISBN 978-1-926715-69-8

The Guilt Cure
by Nancy Carter Pennington & Lawrence H. Staples
1st Ed., Trade Paperback, 200pp, Index, Biblio., 2011
— ISBN 978-1-926715-53-7

Guilt with a Twist: The Promethean Way
by Lawrence Staples,1st Ed., Trade Paperback, 256pp, Index, Biblio., 2008
— ISBN 978-0-9776076-4-8

The Creative Soul: Art and the Quest for Wholeness
by Lawrence Staples, 1st Ed., Trade Paperback, 100pp, Index, Biblio., 2009
— ISBN 978-0-9810344-4-7

Deep Blues: Human Soundscapes for the Archetypal Journey
by Mark Winborn, 1st Ed., Trade Paperback, 130pp, Index, Biblio., 2011
— ISBN 978-1-926715-52-0

Art Therapy Titles

A Salty Lake of Tears: A Soul Journey
by Lois Carey, 1ˢᵗ Ed., Trade Paperback, 112pp, 2011
— ISBN 978-1-926715-47-6

Riting Myth, Mythic Writing
by Dennis Patrick Slattery, 1ˢᵗ Ed., Trade Paperback, 220pp, Biblio., 2012
— ISBN 978-1-926715-77-3

Spirituality/Self-help Titles

Beyond the Mask: The Rising Sign Part 1
by Kathleen Burt – Astrology/Spirituality 1ˢᵗ Ed. Trade Paperback, 170 pp, 2010
— ISBN 978-0-9813939-3-3

Beyond the Mask: The Rising Sign Part 2
by Kathleen Burt – Astrology/Spirituality, 1ˢᵗ Ed. Trade Paperback, 310 pp, 2010
— ISBN 978-0-9813939-9-5

Solar Light, Lunar Light: Perspectives in Human Consciousness
by Howard Teich – Psychology, 1ˢᵗ Ed. Trade Paperback, 120 pp, Index, Biblio., 2012
— ISBN 978-1-926975-05-4

Poetry Titles

Adagio & Lamentation
by Naomi Ruth Lowinsky, 1ˢᵗ Ed. Trade Paperback, 90 pp, 2010
— ISBN 978-1-926715-05-6

After the Jug Was Broken
by Leah Shelleda, 1ˢᵗ Ed. Trade Paperback, 90 pp, 2010
— ISBN 978-1-926715-46-9

Sundered
by Phyllis Stowell 1ˢᵗ Ed. Trade Paperback, 81 pp, 2012
— ISBN 978-1-926715-72-8

Telling the Difference
by Paul Watsky, 1ˢᵗ Ed. Trade Paperback, 81 pp, 2010
— ISBN 978-1-926715-00-1

Plays

Out of the Shadows: A Story of Toni Wolff and Emma Jung
by Elizabeth Clark-Stern, 1st Ed. Trade Paperback, 70 pp, 2010
— ISBN 978-0-9813939-4-0

Nature

Visitation in a Zen Garden
by Karlyn M. Ward, 1st Ed., Trade Paperback, 60pp, illustrated, 2010
— ISBN 978-1-926715-06-3

Literature/Fiction Titles

Timekeeper
by John Atkinson 1st ed Paperback, 200 pp, 2008
— ISBN 978-1-926715-70-4

Dark Shadows Red Bayou
by John Atkinson, Paperback, 200 pp, 2009
— ISBN 978-0-9810344-7-8

Mercy Me
by John Atkinson, Paperback, 80 pp, 2010
— ISBN 978-1-926715-08-7

Timekeeper II
by John Atkinson 1st ed Paperback, 150 pp, 2010
— ISBN 978-1-926715-11-7

Feasts of Phantoms
by Kehinde Ayeni 1st Ed. Paperback, 350 pp, 2010
— ISBN 978-0-9813939-2-6

Journey to the Heart
by Nora Caron, 1st Ed. Paperback, 224 pp, 2008
— ISBN 978-0-9776076-6-2

Soul Stories
by Elizabeth Clark-Stern, 1st Ed. Paperback, 180 pp, 2011
— ISBN 978-1-926975-00-9

Goatsong
by Patricia Damery 1ˢᵗ Ed. Paperback, 180 pp, 2012
—ISBN 978-1-926715-76-6

Snakes
by Patricia Damery, 1ˢᵗ Ed. Paperback, 170 pp, 2011
—ISBN 978-1-926715-13-1

The History of My Body
by Sharon Heath, 1ˢᵗ Ed. Paperback, 300 pp, 2011
— ISBN 978-1-926975-02-3

Main Street Stories
by Phyllis LaPlante, 1ˢᵗ Ed. Paperback, 238 pp, 2010
— ISBN 978-0-9813939-1-9

LeRoi
by Mel Mathews, Rev. Ed. Paperback, 210 pp, 2011
—ISBN 978-1-926715-33-9

Menopause Man—Unplugged
by Mel Mathews, Rev. Ed. Paperback, 270 pp, 2012
—ISBN 978-1-926715-36-0

SamSara
by Mel Mathews, Rev. Ed. Paperback, 280 pp, 2012
—ISBN 978-1-926715-84-1

Requiem: A Tale of Exile & Return
by Erel Shalit, 1ˢᵗ Ed. Paperback, 106 pp, 2010
— ISBN 978-1-926715-03-2

Fisher King Press

Truchas Peaks Place

A Northern New Mexico Retreat & Conference Center

Stunning Natural Beauty • Luxury Accommodations
Meeting & Event Rooms • Wireless Internet

Seminar? Group retreat? Small conference? Family reunion? Are you looking for a unique venue to gather your family or a group of friends? Planning a workshop, an off-site company retreat, or a small wedding? Truchas Peaks Place is the perfect facility for small to mid-size groups, offering exquisite tranquility, luxury bedrooms, meeting rooms, an extensive library, a full-service kitchen for self-catering, and an abundance of possibilities for exploration.

Location, location, location—Truchas Peaks Place is nestled high in the Sangre de Cristo Mountains, with panoramic views of the Truchas Peaks, the Jemez Mountains, and the Pedernal, made famous by Georgia O'Keeffe's paintings. At the midway point between Santa Fe and Taos, we are easily accessible from either city, yet afford the peacefulness and pristine natural surroundings of a secluded retreat. We are part of Spanish colonial village Truchas, settled in 1754 and now a vibrant community of locals of Hispanic origin, artists, and craftspeople. Truchas is a place to go to re-calibrate. To escape stress, city noise, traffic, and everyday worries. To paint, read, walk, think, and spend time with loved ones.

What do you do here? Whatever you want. Draft your next short story. Follow in the footsteps of the many great artists, past and contemporary, who have chosen North Central New Mexico as their base for its inspirational mix of peacefulness and majesty—Truchas is a favorite of poets and writers. Truchas Peaks Place houses the Donald Kalsched – Robin van Loben Sels 10,000-volume library and has more than enough space to allow group members to undertake individual work undisturbed, yet boasts excellent facilities for shared sessions.

Free your inner artist. Sit on the porch at sunset and watch the sun paint the mountains red. The landscape surrounding Truchas would inspire a painter at any skill level to new heights. Why not put together a painting workshop or retreat that includes the annual High Road Art Tour—or your own version of it? Our rich culture and its creative output of sculpture, paintings, photography, pottery, weaving, jewelry, and crafts are sure to inspire you.

Explore the regional cuisine, hands-on style. Try your hand at cooking green chile stew with fresh produce from the farmer's market. The gourmet kitchen at Truchas is the ideal setting for a food-lovers' retreat, a fine cooking workshop, or simply a meal your family will never forget.

Listen to the yipping of the coyotes at dawn. The birds are not the only wild things greeting the stunning morning scenery of North Central New Mexico—though you will find plenty to delight over if bird-watching is a passion of yours. Our state boasts one of the richest lists of resident birds in the nation; around 500 all told. But song-birds share the region with many other animals, from muskrats and turtles to coyotes, deer, and bighorn sheep.

At Truchas, the choices are endless and all yours.

Truchas Peaks Place, 1671 State Road 76, P.O. Box 471, Truchas, NM 87578

www.truchaspeaksplace.com — info@truchaspeaksplace.com

1-866-561-1671

Opus House

A place for Solitude and Creative Work

Opus House is a comfortable adobe home near the old Spanish village of Truchas in the Sangre de Cristo Mountains of Northern New Mexico. Sitting at 8300 feet elevation, 45 minutes from Santa Fe on the High Road to Taos, Opus House is offered to selected individuals of all callings and backgrounds as a place of solitude and creative work. It is seen as a place to be for a week or so to concentrate on a chosen creative process. For those interested in exploring this offering, contact:

Opus House, 1671 State Road 76, P.O. Box 471, Truchas, NM 87578

www.opushouse.org — truchas@opushouse.org

Truchas Learning Center

A Project of the Community for Creative Work, a Non-Profit Organization

The Truchas Learning Center's mission is to provide educational courses in computer literacy, business and the arts to enable students from the rural communities of Northern New Mexico to gain employable skills and become an attractive workforce to American businesses currently sending jobs overseas.

The highly qualified instructors at the Truchas Learning Center are chosen for their expertise and their willingness to donate their teaching time. The founders have sought and received commitments from expert instructors in the fields of computer literacy, computer software design and applications, computer business accounting, computer hardware and networking, Microsoft Office suite, Photoshop, web design, digital media, photography, ethics, and the arts. In exchange for their generosity, the instructors are housed at no charge at the beautiful Truchas Peaks Place Retreat and Conference Center, www.truchaspeaksplace.com or at Opus House, www.opushouse.org

Courses offered by the Truchas Learning Center are at *no charge* to Northern New Mexico students. Long Distance Learning is available in conjunction with local universities and community colleges.

Truchas Learning Center, P.O. Box 442, Truchas, New Mexico 87578
www.truchaslearningcenter.com — info@truchaslearningcenter.com
1-505-689-1112

15425293R00104

Made in the USA
Charleston, SC
02 November 2012